Legends of the Corn Mother and Other Harvest Myths

Legends of the Corn Mother and Other Harvest Myths

Matthew Petchinsky

1

Legends of the Corn Mother and Other Harvest Myths
By: Matthew Petchinsky

Introduction: The Timeless Tale of the Corn Mother and Harvest Myths

Harvest myths have endured through centuries as profound, almost sacred narratives that interlace the human experience with the rhythms of the Earth. At the heart of these myths stands the figure of the Corn Mother, a deity revered across cultures for embodying the very essence of sustenance, fertility, and survival. Her story is not just one tale among many; it is the embodiment of humanity's intricate relationship with nature, the cycles of sowing and reaping, and the profound dance of life, death, and rebirth that characterizes existence itself.

The Universal Significance of Harvest Myths

From the golden wheat fields of ancient Greece to the lush cornfields of the Americas, stories of harvest deities have transcended geographical and temporal boundaries. These myths are far more than tales spun around the hearth; they are reflections of a shared, universal human consciousness that acknowledges the pivotal role of agriculture and sustenance. In many societies, harvest time is synonymous with life itself—a time to celebrate bounty, give thanks, and prepare for the uncertainties of the future.

The Corn Mother, known by different names in various cultures, represents the sacred provider. In Native American traditions, she is often portrayed as the divine matron who sacrificed herself so that humanity could thrive. Her selfless act ensured that people would always have food, symbolizing the ultimate form of nurturing and unconditional love. Similarly, the Greeks revered Demeter, the goddess of the harvest, who embodied maternal care and whose sorrow during the loss of her daughter, Persephone, explained the changing seasons. In both stories, themes of giving, sacrifice, and renewal stand at the forefront, echoing a cycle that every culture understands deeply.

The Impact on Rituals and Traditions

The reverence for harvest deities such as the Corn Mother has influenced countless rituals and traditions throughout history. Festivals, songs, dances, and ceremonies dedicated to the harvest are performed worldwide, each with its own unique interpretation yet rooted in similar themes. These rituals not only celebrate the abundance of food but also serve as reminders of the delicate balance that sustains life. They remind participants of the need for gratitude, community, and stewardship of the land.

For example, in the Native American Green Corn Festival, offerings are made to the Corn Mother in thanks for her sacrifice. This tradition reinforces the belief that life is a continuous cycle of giving and receiving. Across the globe, other harvest festivals—from Lammas in Europe to Pongal in India—emphasize community bonds and collective joy, woven together by the narrative threads of agricultural myths that honor life's cyclical nature.

Life, Death, and Rebirth: Themes Woven in Mythology

One of the most compelling aspects of harvest myths is their inherent focus on the themes of life, death, and rebirth. The Corn Mother's story, for example, often follows a pattern that symbolizes the planting of the seed (life), the withering of the plant (death), and the new growth that follows (rebirth). This cycle serves as a poignant metaphor for the human experience itself—a reminder that endings are not to be feared but are a prelude to new beginnings.

The myths of the Corn Mother and other harvest deities underscore the idea that death is not an absolute finality but a necessary step toward regeneration. These stories echo the seasonal rhythms of nature, where autumn marks a time of harvesting and storing for winter, only for spring to bring about new life. This narrative structure reinforces hope and resilience, even in the face of hardship.

What This Book Offers

In this book, **"Legends of the Corn Mother and Other Harvest Myths,"** we will journey through these timeless stories, delving into their cultural contexts, symbolic meanings, and enduring relevance. Each chapter will explore different harvest myths from around the world, offering a rich tapestry of storytelling and symbolic analysis. Some sections will be presented in the form of vivid, lyrical poetry that aims to capture the ethereal nature of these tales. Other chapters will provide comprehensive explanations of the symbolism embedded in these myths, inviting readers to understand how such stories shape collective beliefs and practices.

Whether you are drawn to the mystical aspects of mythology, the anthropological roots of these stories, or simply appreciate the rich tradition of storytelling, this book is designed to offer something for everyone. It seeks to bridge the past and the present, showing how the wisdom of the Corn Mother and her counterparts continues to inspire rituals, art, and narratives to this day.

Setting the Stage for Exploration

As we embark on this exploration of the Corn Mother and her place in the pantheon of harvest myths, we invite you to see these tales as more than just stories—they are guides that connect humanity to the cycles of the Earth, illustrating our place within the grand scheme of life. With every turn of the page, may you find both the enchantment of ancient legends and the timeless wisdom they impart.

Prepare yourself for a journey filled with the rhythms of nature, poetic passages that capture the soul of each tale, and an analytical lens that reveals the deeper truths embedded in these age-old narratives. From the universal themes of sacrifice and rebirth to the cultural traditions that celebrate these myths, this book promises to be a rich exploration of how the stories of the Corn Mother and other harvest deities continue to resonate with us today.

Chapter 1: The Legend of the Corn Mother

The legend of the Corn Mother is a tale deeply rooted in the spiritual and agricultural life of Native American communities, particularly among the Southeastern tribes. Revered as both a goddess and an ancestral spirit, the Corn Mother embodies the nurturing force that sustains life and provides for the people. Her story, passed down through generations, tells of sacrifice, love, and an eternal bond with the land that feeds and shelters humanity. In this chapter, we will journey through her myth, exploring not only the story itself but also the profound meanings woven into it. Poetic passages will punctuate the narrative, evoking the essence of the Corn Mother and her timeless message.

The Corn Mother's Story: A Tale of Sacrifice and Renewal

In the beginning, before the first stalks of corn ever grew tall under the sun's gaze, the people lived in a time of struggle and hunger. It is said that during this time, a mysterious and radiant woman appeared among them. She was unlike any other, with hair as golden as the summer fields and eyes that held the wisdom of countless harvests. The people came to know her as the Corn Mother, a divine being who possessed the power to bring life to the barren earth.

The Corn Mother was compassionate and wise, seeing the suffering of the people and wishing to help them. She spoke to the elders and taught them the secrets of planting, nurturing, and harvesting the sacred corn. Under her guidance, the once-starving community flourished. Bountiful crops rose from the soil, offering sustenance that carried them through harsh seasons. Corn was not just food; it was a gift of the spirit, a symbol of life, fertility, and the interconnectedness of the people with nature.

But as with many legends, the tale of the Corn Mother carries a profound theme of sacrifice. One version of the story recounts how the Corn Mother revealed to the people that her life would be needed to ensure that the gift of corn would remain forever. Knowing that her departure would be mourned, she comforted the people, promising that her spirit would always dwell within the corn they harvested.

Poetic Passage: A Song of the Corn Mother

Golden-haired mother, gentle and wise,
With earth's bounty held in your embrace,
You walk among us, seed of the skies,
And in your touch, we find our place.

Your whispers teach the soil to yield,
Each grain a story, each stalk a song.
From tender roots to the sunlit field,
You are the spirit that makes us strong.

The Sacrifice and Transformation

The most poignant part of the Corn Mother's myth is the moment of her sacrifice. In one version of the story, she lays down upon the soil, allowing her body to transform into the crops that would sustain the people for generations. As she fades, the wind carries her voice: "Take of me, and live. From my essence, you shall always find nourishment."

In another variation, the Corn Mother requests that the people gather her remains and bury them in the fertile soil. Reluctantly, they comply, weeping as they perform the solemn act. From the place where her body was laid, the first corn sprouts emerged, golden and swaying, as if touched by a divine breath. The people marveled at this miracle and understood that the Corn Mother's promise was true. Though she had left them in form, her spirit had not departed. She remained with them, growing with each stalk and nourishing them with every meal.

This tale encapsulates the cycle of life, death, and rebirth—a theme echoed in countless cultures that recognize the rhythms of the natural world. The sacrifice of the Corn Mother is a reminder that life's sustenance often requires an offering, a reminder that abundance and gratitude are inextricably linked.

Poetic Passage: The Sacrifice

Oh, mother of harvest, in earth you lay,
Your gift of life, a price you paid,
Through tender roots, your soul shall stay,
And in each kernel, your love conveyed.

We mourned you in silence, earth's embrace,
But soon the soil, it whispered sweet,
And there you rose, in golden grace,
Your spirit, now our hearts' heartbeat.

The Corn Mother as the Embodiment of Nature's Cycle

The story of the Corn Mother is more than a recounting of how a sacred plant came to be; it is a lesson in reciprocity and stewardship. Native American tribes often treated the cultivation and consumption of corn with rituals of respect and gratitude. Ceremonies would include dances, chants, and prayers, offered to honor the spirit of the Corn Mother who continued to provide for them long after her earthly sacrifice.

The Corn Mother symbolizes the deep respect for the interconnected web of life, where taking from nature is always met with a promise to nurture and protect in return. This balance between giving and receiving, sacrifice and gain, is at the heart of sustainable living. To this day, many indigenous communities perform the Green Corn Ceremony, a festival of renewal, gratitude, and purification. It is a sacred time when the bond between the people and the Corn Mother is honored through acts of devotion and celebration.

The Spiritual Legacy of the Corn Mother

The spiritual significance of the Corn Mother extends beyond her role as a provider of sustenance. She is an archetype of the Great Mother, representing the nurturing force present in all life. Her myth is a reminder that abundance comes not just from the seeds we sow in the ground, but from the seeds of kindness, sacrifice, and community we plant in our lives. The Corn Mother teaches that true wealth is found not in hoarding what we have but in sharing it freely, knowing that it will return to us in many forms.

In the teachings of the Corn Mother, there is an understanding that life is a sacred cycle. Her myth teaches that every harvest is a culmination of hard work, respect for the land, and the remembrance of those who made it possible. Through her story, we see that even in loss, there is renewal, and in death, a promise of rebirth.

Poetic Passage: Eternal Renewal

From ashes and earth, your gift is born,
A cycle that turns with sun and moon,
In every harvest, we find the morn,
Of sacrifice's sacred boon.

Corn Mother, spirit of golden grain,
Keeper of cycles, ancient and deep,
With each feast, we honor your reign,
And in your memory, our promise we keep.

Conclusion: The Seeds of Understanding

The story of the Corn Mother is not just a piece of folklore; it is a symbol of the values that underpin human connection with the natural world. It is a reminder of gratitude, sacrifice, and the sacredness of giving back to what sustains us. As we move forward through this book, exploring the myriad harvest myths from cultures around the world, the legend of the Corn Mother will serve as a guiding light. Her legacy is one that transcends time, speaking to the universal human experience of growth, loss, and the hope of renewal.

In honoring the Corn Mother's story, we find the seeds of understanding that continue to grow within us, cultivating a deeper appreciation for the gifts of the Earth and the cycles that sustain life itself.

Chapter 2: The Spirit of the Harvest

The spirit of the harvest is a theme that spans the globe, woven into the folklore, traditions, and beliefs of countless indigenous cultures. At the heart of these beliefs lies the idea that the harvest is not just a natural process but a sacred act guided by spiritual forces. The Corn Mother, as explored in the previous chapter, stands as a prominent embodiment of this idea. However, the mythologies and rituals surrounding the harvest spirit extend beyond the Native American tribes and resonate with numerous parallels and contrasts in cultures worldwide.

This chapter will explore the personification of the harvest in various indigenous traditions, drawing comparisons with the Corn Mother and delving into the symbolic analysis of her role in the cyclical dance of planting and reaping. By examining these similarities and distinctions, we gain a more profound understanding of how humanity has universally revered the harvest as both a gift and a responsibility.

The Harvest Deities: Parallels and Contrasts

The Andean Pachamama: Earth Mother and Provider

In the Andean regions of South America, Pachamama is revered as the goddess of the earth and fertility. Much like the Corn Mother, Pachamama embodies both the nurturing and sustaining aspects of the land. She is more than a symbol of agriculture; she represents the interconnectedness of life, linking humans to the earth and ensuring their survival through the gifts of nature. The people of the Andes celebrate rituals to honor Pachamama, particularly during the harvest season. Offerings, or *despachos*, are prepared with symbolic items such as coca leaves, seeds, and small models of crops and livestock, expressing gratitude and requesting her blessing for future abundance.

The parallels between Pachamama and the Corn Mother are evident in their shared roles as maternal figures who provide sustenance and symbolize the cycle of life. Yet, there are contrasts as well. While the Corn Mother's myth emphasizes personal sacrifice and transformation, Pachamama is seen more as an enduring presence who must be appeased and respected to ensure continuous bounty. Where the Corn Mother's story involves a profound act of giving that shapes her people's existence, Pachamama's narrative focuses on balance and reciprocity with the earth.

Demeter: The Greek Goddess of the Harvest

Demeter, the Greek goddess of the harvest and fertility, is another parallel to the Corn Mother. Her story is famously tied to that of her daughter Persephone and the cycle of the seasons. When Persephone was abducted by Hades and taken to the underworld, Demeter's grief was so great that the earth ceased to yield crops, plunging the world into a barren winter. Only when Persephone was allowed to return for part of the year did Demeter's joy bring the land back to life, marking the arrival of spring and the renewal of growth.

The myth of Demeter is rich with symbolism, echoing the themes of life, death, and rebirth found in the Corn Mother's story. Both figures demonstrate the profound emotional and spiritual connection between the harvest and human life. However, while the Corn Mother embodies the harvest through her direct transformation into the life-giving corn, Demeter represents the impact of loss and reunion on the earth's fertility, emphasizing a more emotional and relational aspect of the cycle.

The African Oshun: Fertility and Abundance

In Yoruba tradition, Oshun is the orisha (deity) of fresh water, fertility, and abundance. Although not directly tied to agriculture like the Corn Mother, Oshun plays an essential role in nurturing life and ensuring prosperity. Her presence is vital for crops to grow and for the land to be fertile, symbolizing the balance needed to maintain abundance. Ceremonies dedicated to Oshun involve offerings and dances performed by her devotees, who seek her blessings for prosperity, healing, and joy.

Oshun's symbolic connection to water differentiates her from the Corn Mother but also highlights the universal recognition of nature's cycles and their dependency on spiritual forces. Where the Corn Mother's myth centers on sacrifice and regeneration, Oshun's story emphasizes celebration, pleasure, and the life-giving force of water. Both deities, however, underscore the theme of nurturing and the sacredness of life's sustenance.

Symbolic Analysis: The Role of the Corn Mother in the Cycle of Planting and Harvest

The Corn Mother's story is rich with symbolism that transcends her literal role as the origin of corn. Her presence in the cycle of planting and harvest embodies deeper themes that resonate across cultures and time.

The Cycle of Sacrifice and Renewal

At its core, the Corn Mother's story is one of sacrifice. Her willingness to give her life to feed her people reflects the belief that life's abundance often requires an offering. This concept is mirrored in many indigenous practices where the earth is respected as a living entity, and harvests are seen as gifts that come at a cost. The Corn Mother's act of self-sacrifice becomes a ritualistic reminder that gratitude and reverence must accompany every act of reaping. In her transformation—from a nurturing figure to the crops that sustain the tribe—lies the message that death is not an end but a transformation that gives birth to new life.

This cycle is central to the agricultural rituals of many cultures, where planting is seen as a sacred act. Seeds are laid into the earth, mirroring burial, only to rise again as life-giving plants. The Corn Mother embodies this cyclical truth, teaching that all life is interconnected and that renewal requires a return to the source.

The Feminine Divine as Sustainer

The Corn Mother represents the feminine divine as the sustainer of life. She is the archetypal Mother Earth, holding the power of creation, nourishment, and resilience. In many indigenous cultures, the role of women in agricultural societies echoes this divine archetype. Women often play key roles in planting, harvesting, and preparing food, reflecting their vital connection to life's cycles. The Corn Mother's story reinforces this sacred association, reminding communities that the feminine force is integral to survival and prosperity.

This connection is further illustrated in rituals that involve women leading ceremonies or performing songs and dances to honor the harvest. The presence of the feminine in these acts highlights the Corn Mother's symbolic role in ensuring that the community remains in harmony with the rhythms of nature.

Themes of Community and Reciprocity

The Corn Mother's tale is not just about the relationship between humanity and the earth but also about the interconnectedness of people within a community. Her sacrifice is not a solitary act; it is for the benefit of the entire tribe. This theme underscores the importance of reciprocity—not only with the land but among people. Indigenous cultures often emphasize the collective nature of survival, where each individual's wellbeing is tied to the wellbeing of others.

Ceremonial practices surrounding the harvest often involve communal participation. Feasts, dances, and songs are shared experiences, binding the community through shared gratitude and celebration. The Corn Mother's legacy teaches that abundance is a collective gift and should be received with humility and shared generously.

Parallels Across Cultures: A Shared Reverence

The idea of a divine or semi-divine figure associated with the harvest is a near-universal concept. Whether it is Pachamama, Demeter, or Oshun, the parallels to the Corn Mother reveal a shared human understanding: that life is sustained through a delicate balance of giving and taking, nurturing and being nurtured. These deities serve as reminders that the act of harvest is as much a spiritual act as it is a physical one.

Poetic Passage: The Spirit of the Harvest

Spirit of grain, spirit of rain,
Mother who gives, yet takes again.
In every seed, your voice is heard,
In whispered wind, your silent word.
We plant, we pray, and then we reap,
With offerings made, promises keep.
Through cycles worn, your tale we tell,
In harvest's heart, we know you well.

Conclusion: The Living Spirit of Abundance

The Corn Mother and other harvest deities remind us that the act of harvesting is a sacred contract between humanity and the earth. Their stories are more than mere folklore; they are teachings that guide how we interact with the natural world. The Corn Mother's narrative is one of profound gratitude, sacrifice, and the continuous cycle of renewal. As we explore more harvest myths in the coming chapters, the spirit of the Corn Mother will continue to serve as a touchstone, embodying the eternal balance of life, death, and rebirth that has connected cultures across millennia.

Chapter 3: Ceres and the Roman Bounty

Ceres, the Roman goddess of agriculture, grain crops, fertility, and motherly relationships, embodies the spirit of the harvest and the sustenance it provides. Her mythology, intertwined with the tale of her daughter Proserpina, weaves a rich narrative of loss, love, and renewal that has deeply influenced Roman art, culture, and religious practices. In this chapter, we will delve into the legend of Ceres and Proserpina, explore its symbolic meanings, and analyze its significant impact on Roman life and its enduring presence in art and cultural expressions.

The Story of Ceres and Proserpina: A Tale of Loss and Love

Ceres' story begins in a time of peace and prosperity when she was revered by the Roman people as the provider of grain and agricultural wealth. She nurtured the earth, ensuring that fields were fertile and crops thrived. Ceres' daughter, Proserpina, was the light of her life, embodying the beauty and innocence of youth. The bond between mother and daughter was profound, symbolizing an unbreakable connection that reflected the vital relationship between life and its source.

The harmony of their world was shattered when Pluto, the god of the underworld, caught sight of Proserpina and was captivated by her beauty. Consumed by desire, he seized her and took her to his shadowy realm to make her his queen. Proserpina's sudden disappearance plunged Ceres into grief so deep that it disrupted the natural order. In her anguish, she wandered the earth, neglecting her duties, and as a result, the fields withered, crops failed, and famine loomed over humanity.

Poetic Passage: The Weeping Mother

Oh, Ceres, goddess of the grain,
With eyes that weep the falling rain,
You search the earth for what was taken,
A mother's heart, now lost and shaken.

Your grief turns fields from green to gray,
And in the sun's light, shadows play.
The world stands still, its breath withheld,
As sorrow's silence is deeply felt.

The Search and the Plea

Ceres' search for Proserpina led her across mountains, forests, and rivers, but she found no trace of her daughter. In desperation, she approached the king of the gods, Jupiter, pleading for help. Moved by Ceres' despair and the plight of the starving humans, Jupiter intervened and demanded that Pluto return Proserpina. However, a divine law decreed that if Proserpina had consumed any food from the underworld, she would be bound to it forever. Alas, Proserpina had eaten six pomegranate seeds, sealing her fate.

Jupiter proposed a compromise: Proserpina would spend six months of the year with Pluto as queen of the underworld and the remaining six months with Ceres. This arrangement brought about the cycle of the seasons. When Proserpina was with her mother, the earth flourished in spring and summer, symbolizing renewal and joy. When she returned to the underworld, Ceres' grief returned, marking the barren months of autumn and winter.

Symbolic Analysis: Life, Death, and Renewal

The myth of Ceres and Proserpina encapsulates the cycle of life, death, and rebirth—a theme that echoes across cultures and remains deeply symbolic in Roman society. Ceres, as a maternal figure, represents the nurturing aspect of nature, while Proserpina embodies both the innocence of life and the inevitability of death. The pomegranate seeds that bind Proserpina to the underworld symbolize the acceptance of fate and the duality of existence.

The Seasonal Cycle

The myth explains the changing of the seasons and serves as a metaphor for the human experience. Spring and summer, marked by Proserpina's return to Ceres, symbolize life, growth, and abundance. Autumn and winter, when Proserpina resides with Pluto, symbolize death, dormancy, and the trials that precede renewal. This allegory reinforces the idea that periods of darkness and suffering are temporary and lead to the eventual rebirth of joy and abundance.

The ritual celebrations in ancient Rome, such as the *Ambarvalia* and the festival of *Cerealia*, honored this cycle. These festivities involved offerings of grain and other produce to Ceres, communal feasting, and processions, symbolizing gratitude for the goddess' gifts and invoking her blessings for future harvests.

The Influence of Ceres' Myth on Art and Culture

The story of Ceres and Proserpina has left an indelible mark on Roman art, literature, and religious practice. Ceres was depicted in numerous statues and reliefs, often holding a cornucopia, a symbol of abundance, or sheaves of wheat, emphasizing her role as the nurturer of the earth. Temples dedicated to Ceres were common, with the most significant being the *Temple of Ceres, Liber, and Libera* on the Aventine Hill in Rome, serving as a place of worship and a hub for the *plebeians* who relied heavily on agriculture.

Literature and Poetry

Roman poets such as Ovid and Virgil immortalized the tale of Ceres and Proserpina in their works. Ovid's *Metamorphoses* details the emotional journey of Ceres, offering vivid imagery of her sorrow and the impact of her search on the world. The story's themes resonated so deeply that it became a cornerstone of Roman and later Western literature, symbolizing the balance between grief and hope, loss and recovery.

Virgil's *Georgics* also reflects the influence of Ceres in its celebration of agricultural life and the relationship between humans and the divine forces governing nature. Through these literary works, Ceres' story became a cultural touchstone, emphasizing the importance of resilience and renewal.

Visual Arts and Symbolism

The visual representation of Ceres and Proserpina's myth can be found in mosaics, frescoes, and sculptures throughout ancient Rome. Artists depicted the moment of Proserpina's abduction, Ceres' anguished search, and the joyful reunion that heralded the return of spring. The image of Ceres holding a torch, searching tirelessly for her daughter, became a powerful symbol of hope and the relentless pursuit of love and justice.

One of the most famous artistic representations is the *Rape of Proserpina* by Gian Lorenzo Bernini, created in the Baroque era. Although crafted long after the fall of Rome, this sculpture captures the raw emotion of Proserpina's abduction, emphasizing the enduring power of the myth and its ability to inspire awe and empathy through generations.

Ceres in Roman Religious Practices

Ceres was central to Roman religious life, particularly among the agrarian population. The *Cerealia*, celebrated in April, was one of the most important festivals dedicated to her. The event included theatrical performances, games, and rituals designed to invoke Ceres' blessings on the crops and ensure a prosperous harvest. Participants offered sacrifices, such as pigs and first fruits, to honor the goddess and express gratitude for her protection and providence.

The connection between Ceres and the Roman plebeians was especially significant. As the protectress of the lower classes who toiled the land, Ceres was more than a divine figure; she was an advocate for the working masses. This made her worship not just a spiritual practice but a social statement that reinforced the bond between the people and the sustenance they relied on.

Poetic Passage: The Return of Proserpina

From shadow's grip, she rises bright,
A daughter claimed, restored to light.
In fields and flowers, joy's refrain,
As Ceres holds her close again.
The earth awakens, green and bold,
As tales of grief and love unfold.
Renewal's touch, the world reclaims,
And spring returns, with whispered names.

Conclusion: The Eternal Influence of Ceres

The legend of Ceres and Proserpina stands as a powerful narrative of love, loss, and renewal that has permeated Roman culture and extended its influence throughout history. This myth, while grounded in the agricultural cycle, is a profound commentary on the human condition and the enduring hope that follows sorrow. Ceres' role as the maternal figure who brings life and ensures rebirth resonates with the universal experience of grief and the anticipation of joy's return.

As we continue to explore other harvest deities and their stories, the tale of Ceres and Proserpina will serve as a reminder of the complex relationships between gods and mortals, nature and society, and the cyclical dance that binds life, death, and renewal in an eternal embrace.

Chapter 4: Demeter and Persephone

The myth of Demeter and Persephone is one of the most poignant and enduring stories from Greek mythology, weaving together themes of love, loss, and renewal. This tale not only serves as an allegory for the changing of the seasons but also embodies profound symbolic meanings related to motherhood, fertility, and the cyclical nature of life. Demeter, the goddess of the harvest and agriculture, and her daughter Persephone, whose abduction by Hades brought profound sorrow to her mother, personify the eternal balance between life and death, growth and dormancy. In this chapter, we will explore the rich details of their story, interpret its symbols, and uncover the ways it has shaped cultural understandings of nature and the sacred feminine.

The Story of Demeter and Persephone: A Myth of Love and Loss

Demeter, one of the twelve Olympian deities, was revered as the goddess of the harvest, fertility, and the nurturing aspects of motherhood. Her daughter, Persephone, was the product of her union with Zeus, and together they shared an unbreakable bond. Persephone was known for her beauty and innocence, often depicted as a maiden frolicking in the fields of eternal spring, where flowers bloomed perpetually.

The serenity of their life was shattered when Hades, the god of the underworld, caught sight of Persephone and was immediately captivated by her. With the consent of Zeus but without Demeter's knowledge, Hades emerged from the depths of his dark realm and carried Persephone away in his chariot. Her cries echoed across the earth, reaching the ears of her mother, but not soon enough for Demeter to save her.

Demeter's Grief and the Withering Earth

Demeter's anguish upon discovering that Persephone was missing was profound. She roamed the earth in despair, abandoning her divine duties and searching tirelessly for her daughter. The fields, once lush and fertile under her care, began to wither, and a great famine spread over the land. Without Demeter's nurturing touch, crops failed, and the once-thriving world faced starvation and ruin. This decline symbolized the earth's mourning in harmony with Demeter's pain—a reflection of the deep connection between the goddess and the natural world.

For days and nights, Demeter searched, holding a torch aloft as she wandered in desperation. Her grief was so immense that even the gods began to fear the consequences of her despair. Mortals and immortals alike felt the weight of her sorrow, as the earth became cold and barren. The harvest goddess refused to let anything grow until her beloved daughter was returned to her.

Poetic Passage: The Search of the Goddess

Demeter roams with tear-streaked face,
A torch in hand, in frantic chase.
The land, once green, now dry and pale,
Echoes her grief, her mournful wail.

Oh, daughter lost to shadow's hold,
Return to warmth, forsake the cold.
For in your absence, life does cease,
And only sorrow finds release.

The Compromise and the Cycle of the Seasons

Demeter's relentless search eventually led her to Helios, the all-seeing god of the sun, who revealed the truth: Hades had taken Persephone to be his queen. Upon hearing this, Demeter's grief turned to fury. She confronted Zeus, demanding the return of her daughter, and threatened to let the earth remain barren if her wish was not granted. Faced with the potential extinction of humankind, Zeus sent Hermes, the swift messenger god, to negotiate Persephone's release.

Hades, although reluctant, agreed to let Persephone go, but he had a final trick to ensure she would return: before she left, he offered her pomegranate seeds. Persephone, unaware of the consequences, ate six seeds. This act bound her to the underworld for a portion of each year, as consuming food from Hades' realm meant a soul was forever linked to it.

The agreement reached was bittersweet: Persephone would spend six months with her mother on the earth, during which Demeter's joy would bring forth spring and summer, times of growth and abundance. For the other six months, Persephone would return to the underworld, and Demeter's sorrow would cast the world into the dormancy of autumn and winter. This cycle explained the changing of the seasons, linking the myth to the natural transitions between fertility and decline.

Poetic Passage: The Return and Parting

From shadowed halls to fields of light,
Persephone ascends, a welcome sight.
Her mother's arms, a shelter wide,
Restore the earth in joy and pride.

But soon the seeds, their claim make known,
And back she goes, to sit on a throne.
Thus winter falls, with silent breath,
A time of waiting, a taste of death.

Symbolic Interpretations: Motherhood, Fertility, and Duality

The myth of Demeter and Persephone is layered with symbolic meanings that resonate with universal human experiences. At its heart, it is a story of motherhood, the powerful bond between a mother and child, and the lengths to which a mother will go to protect and reunite with her offspring. Demeter's grief is a reflection of the natural world's response to loss, while her joy upon Persephone's return symbolizes renewal and rebirth.

Motherhood and Unconditional Love

Demeter's unwavering love for Persephone illustrates the archetype of the Great Mother, an embodiment of nurturing, protection, and sacrifice. This maternal force is not just present in the biological sense but represents the sustaining energy that supports life itself. Demeter's refusal to allow growth during her daughter's absence underscores the idea that without the love and care of the mother figure, life cannot flourish.

Fertility and the Life Cycle

The cycle of life and death is central to Demeter's myth. Her grief during Persephone's absence aligns with the barrenness of winter, a season when life retreats and growth ceases. The return of Persephone, bringing joy and abundance, symbolizes spring and summer, times of fertility and plenty. This cyclical pattern reflects the agricultural calendar, where sowing, growth, harvest, and rest are natural stages that sustain human life. Demeter's influence as the goddess of agriculture reinforces the understanding that fertility is both a physical and spiritual process, connected to the rhythms of nature.

Duality and Transformation

Persephone's dual existence as the queen of the underworld and the daughter of the harvest goddess represents the concept of duality. She embodies both life and death, innocence and wisdom. Her transformation from a carefree maiden to a sovereign queen signifies the transition from youth to maturity, a theme that speaks to personal growth and acceptance of life's complexities. Persephone's consumption of the pomegranate seeds is symbolic of choice and consequence, marking her acceptance of her role as the bridge between two worlds.

The Influence on Art and Culture

The myth of Demeter and Persephone has left an indelible mark on art, literature, and culture throughout history. Ancient Greek pottery often depicted scenes of the mother and daughter in moments of reunion or parting, capturing the emotional weight of their relationship.

The Eleusinian Mysteries, one of the most significant religious rites of ancient Greece, were dedicated to Demeter and Persephone, symbolizing the hope of rebirth and the promise of life after death. Initiates to these mysteries were said to gain secret knowledge that promised spiritual renewal and a deeper understanding of the cycles of existence.

Literature and Drama

Greek playwrights and poets, including Homer, Hesiod, and later, Ovid, explored the story of Demeter and Persephone in their works. Homer's *Homeric Hymn to Demeter* is one of the most comprehensive sources of the myth, capturing the goddess' sorrow, her search, and the ultimate resolution. Ovid's *Metamorphoses* adds layers of poetic interpretation, focusing on themes of transformation and the eternal dance between light and darkness.

Renaissance and Beyond

During the Renaissance, artists and writers revisited classical mythology with renewed interest. Painters such as Sandro Botticelli depicted scenes inspired by the myth, infusing them with allegorical and humanist interpretations. In the Baroque period, works like *The Rape of Persephone* by Gian Lorenzo Bernini evoked powerful emotions and captured the dramatic intensity of the abduction, blending classical mythology with the expressive style of the era.

Poetic Passage: The Changing of the Seasons

The earth reflects a mother's woe,
As autumn's chill and winter's snow
Mark time until the warmth returns,
And Ceres' heart no longer yearns.

With spring, a daughter's laughter rings,
And summer's dance, a joy it brings.
But always looms the shadow's call,
A cycle turning, one and all.

Conclusion: A Legacy of Resilience and Renewal

The story of Demeter and Persephone is more than a myth explaining the seasons; it is a powerful allegory of resilience, motherhood, and the duality inherent in life. Demeter's grief teaches us that loss is an inevitable part of existence, while her reunion with Persephone reminds us that joy and renewal are just as certain. This myth encapsulates the essence of life's cycles, mirroring the natural world's periods of growth and dormancy and reinforcing the idea that even in the depths of winter, the promise of spring endures.

As we continue to explore other myths and legends of the harvest, the tale of Demeter and Persephone will serve as a cornerstone, illustrating the profound ways in which stories shape our understanding of nature, the sacred feminine, and the enduring human spirit.

Chapter 5: The Rice Goddess Dewi Sri

In the lush, emerald landscapes of Indonesia, where rice is the lifeblood of the people, Dewi Sri stands as a central figure in mythology. Revered as the goddess of rice, fertility, and prosperity, Dewi Sri's story is woven into the cultural fabric of Indonesian life. Her influence is seen not just in religious rituals but in the daily practices and beliefs that surround the planting, harvesting, and consumption of rice. This chapter will explore the mythology of Dewi Sri, capturing the essence of her divine attributes, her stories, and the symbolic significance she holds as the guardian of rice fields. Additionally, we will present a poem that embodies her celestial beauty and nurturing presence.

The Mythology of Dewi Sri: Life, Sacrifice, and Abundance

Dewi Sri's story originates from ancient Javanese and Sundanese cultures, which view her as the most important deity related to rice and agricultural fertility. Rice, being a staple of Indonesian diets and a critical economic resource, is considered sacred, and Dewi Sri's divine connection to it elevates her status to that of a goddess who must be honored and revered.

According to one of the most well-known myths, Dewi Sri was born from the union of the sky god Batara Guru and his wife. Her arrival was marked by a radiant light, signifying her divine nature. Dewi Sri was not only beautiful but compassionate and wise, embodying all the qualities of a nurturing mother and provider. Her presence was said to bring fertility and prosperity to the land, ensuring the growth of rice and the survival of the people.

The Sacrifice of Dewi Sri

One of the most poignant aspects of Dewi Sri's story involves her ultimate sacrifice. In one version of the myth, Dewi Sri was pursued by the god Antaboga, a serpent deity who wished to possess her. Fearing for her safety, she sought refuge on earth. During her time among humans, Dewi Sri brought them the knowledge of rice cultivation, teaching them how to plant, harvest, and sustain themselves. Her teachings were sacred and quickly became the foundation of agricultural life.

However, Dewi Sri's time on earth was not meant to last. When the gods discovered her absence from the heavens, they demanded her return. Unwilling to leave her beloved humans without the sustenance she had provided, Dewi Sri chose to sacrifice her mortal form so that rice, a life-giving crop, could continue to grow. Her body transformed into rice plants, and her spirit imbued them with her divine essence. This act of selflessness immortalized Dewi Sri as the eternal protector of the rice fields, ensuring that her nurturing presence would always be with her people.

Poetic Passage: The Sacrifice of Dewi Sri

From heavens high, a goddess came,
With eyes of light and voice aflame.
She walked the fields, with tender grace,
And taught the earth her sacred pace.

But when the gods called her away,
And shadows loomed to bid her stay,
She gave herself, with whispered might,
To be the seed, the grain, the light.

Now in each stalk, her spirit dwells,
A tale of love that nature tells.
For every harvest, songs are sung,
Of Dewi Sri, forever young.

The Symbolic Significance of Dewi Sri

Dewi Sri's mythology is rich with symbols that resonate deeply with the agricultural and spiritual lives of the Indonesian people. Her story is not just a tale of divine intervention but a representation of essential themes such as sacrifice, renewal, and the sacred connection between humans and the earth.

Fertility and Motherhood

As a fertility goddess, Dewi Sri embodies the nurturing, motherly aspects of life. Her image is often depicted with flowing hair, adorned in intricate garments, and holding a bundle of rice stalks or an earthen vessel, symbolizing her role as the provider of nourishment. Temples and shrines dedicated to her are common in rice fields and village centers, serving as places where offerings of flowers, rice, and incense are made to seek her blessings for a bountiful harvest.

Dewi Sri's story mirrors the deep respect that Indonesian culture holds for motherhood and the role of women in maintaining family and community life. The rice goddess is seen as the divine mother whose presence ensures the fertility of the fields, thereby supporting the cycle of life. This connection to maternal energy reinforces the belief that nature is a living, nurturing force deserving of respect and reverence.

The Sacredness of Rice

Rice is more than just a crop in Indonesia; it is a sacred gift. The belief that Dewi Sri's spirit resides within each grain elevates the act of rice cultivation to a religious duty. Planting and harvesting rituals are carried out with deep respect, as these practices are considered acts of devotion. The rice goddess's influence permeates every stage of the agricultural process, from the initial planting to the harvest and eventual consumption. The first harvest is often dedicated to her, accompanied by festivals that include dance, song, and prayers of gratitude.

The rituals performed in honor of Dewi Sri emphasize the interconnectedness of the human and divine realms. By acknowledging her role in providing sustenance, the community expresses gratitude and seeks her continued favor, reinforcing a relationship based on respect, reciprocity, and shared prosperity.

Sacrifice and Transformation

The story of Dewi Sri's sacrifice highlights the theme of transformation and the belief that life often requires acts of giving. Just as Dewi Sri transformed her body into rice to ensure the survival of humanity, so too does the cycle of planting and harvest involve transformation. Seeds are planted, nurtured, and eventually cut down to provide nourishment, only to be replanted once more. This cycle reflects the goddess's gift and serves as a reminder of the continuous exchange between humanity and nature.

The idea that life comes from sacrifice is a common theme in agricultural myths around the world. Dewi Sri's willingness to become one with the rice plants symbolizes the ultimate act of love and commitment to the well-being of her people. It teaches that prosperity is not achieved without giving something of oneself, reinforcing the cultural value of selflessness and collective welfare.

Celebrations and Rituals: Honoring Dewi Sri

The reverence for Dewi Sri is evident in numerous celebrations and rituals conducted throughout Indonesia. The *Sedekah Bumi* (Earth Offering) and *Nyadran* are traditional ceremonies where villagers come together to offer thanks for the harvest and pray for future abundance. These rituals often involve music, dances performed in elaborate costumes, and processions to sacred sites. The offerings typically include rice, fruits, flowers, and symbolic items that represent fertility and abundance.

In Javanese culture, the *Ruwatan* ceremony is sometimes performed to cleanse and purify the rice fields and surrounding environment, ensuring that Dewi Sri's favor is maintained. This ceremony serves to remind the community of their dependence on the land and the goddess who watches over it. It reinforces the belief that harmony between the physical and spiritual realms is essential for continued prosperity.

Poetic Passage: The Guardian of the Fields

Dewi Sri, with gentle smile,
You walk the rows, each ear beguile.
In sun and rain, your spirit sways,
And guides the farmers' humble ways.

Your touch is found in verdant green,
Where rice fields whisper, bright and serene.
Protector, mother, source divine,
Through you, the earth and stars align.

When harvest comes, and scythes do sing,
We honor you, eternal spring.
A grain of rice, a gift so small,
Yet holds your heart, the life of all.

The Enduring Legacy of Dewi Sri

Dewi Sri's story continues to resonate in modern Indonesia, where traditional beliefs coexist with contemporary life. Her myth is taught to children, performed in dances, and depicted in art, ensuring that her legacy as the protector of rice and symbol of fertility endures. Even in urban settings, the reverence for Dewi Sri remains a part of cultural identity, reminding people of their connection to the land and the values of gratitude, sacrifice, and mutual care.

Dewi Sri's presence also highlights the deep-rooted environmental consciousness inherent in Indonesian culture. The respect for the rice goddess extends to a broader appreciation for nature and the understanding that humanity's survival depends on nurturing the earth as she nurtures her people. By keeping her memory alive, communities reaffirm their commitment to maintaining balance and harmony with the natural world.

Conclusion: A Symbol of Eternal Nurture

Dewi Sri's mythology is more than just a tale; it is an expression of the values and beliefs that sustain the Indonesian way of life. Her story of sacrifice and transformation, her role as the divine protector of rice fields, and the cultural rituals that honor her embody the sacred relationship between humans and the earth. Dewi Sri teaches that abundance is a shared blessing, cultivated through love, respect, and selflessness.

As we explore further into the myths of harvest deities across the world, the story of Dewi Sri serves as a reminder of the universal recognition that nature's gifts are both a privilege and a responsibility. Her legacy continues to inspire a sense of gratitude and stewardship, celebrating the divine cycle of growth, nourishment, and renewal that sustains all life.

Chapter 6: Ancestral Roots in European Folklore

European folklore is replete with rich and varied traditions that center around the themes of harvest, fertility, and the cycles of nature. At the heart of these beliefs are harvest deities who embody the nurturing spirit of the land and the community's dependence on the natural world for sustenance. Among these deities, the Slavic goddess Mokosh and the Norse goddess Sif stand out as powerful figures who shaped not only religious practices but also agrarian life. This chapter will delve into the stories and attributes of these goddesses, exploring the symbolic connections between their myths and the agricultural practices of their respective cultures.

The Slavic Goddess Mokosh: The Protector of Women and Harvests

In Slavic mythology, Mokosh is revered as a goddess of fertility, the earth, and women's crafts, embodying the dual roles of life-giver and protector. Her name is often associated with moisture, linking her to the nurturing power of water, essential for both the fertility of the land and human life. Mokosh is one of the oldest deities in the Slavic pantheon, and her influence extends across agricultural and domestic spheres.

The Attributes of Mokosh

Mokosh is depicted as a matronly figure, with long hair symbolizing her connection to the fertile earth and the cycle of life. She is often shown holding tools such as a spindle or sheaves of grain, emphasizing her role in both nurturing crops and overseeing the household activities of spinning and weaving. This portrayal underscores her dual connection to the land and to the vital role of women in maintaining the home and supporting agricultural efforts.

Mokosh's association with fertility and moisture made her indispensable in rituals that sought to ensure a good harvest. Prayers and offerings were made to her before the planting and harvesting seasons, seeking her blessing for rain and bountiful crops. The practice of leaving small tokens, such as pieces of cloth or bread, at sacred sites dedicated to Mokosh was common, reflecting the deep-seated belief that her favor was crucial for the community's survival.

Symbolic Analysis: Life, Death, and Regeneration

Mokosh's role as a fertility goddess places her at the center of the cycle of life, death, and regeneration. This cycle is mirrored in the agrarian practices of the Slavs, who viewed the sowing and reaping of crops as sacred acts infused with the goddess's presence. Just as seeds are buried in the soil to later rise as life-giving plants, Mokosh's influence signifies the transformative power of the earth. Her name, connected to moisture, reinforces the idea that life requires nurturing and protection.

Mokosh also embodies the resilience of the natural world. In many tales, she is seen as a figure who safeguards not just crops but also the well-being of women, symbolizing the interconnectedness of human life and nature's cycles. This duality speaks to the importance of community and shared responsibility, as the health of the land was inextricably linked to the health of the people.

The Norse Goddess Sif: The Golden-Haired Symbol of Fertility

In Norse mythology, Sif is renowned as the goddess of fertility, the harvest, and the hearth. Her most distinctive attribute is her golden hair, which is often interpreted as a symbol of ripe wheat fields and the wealth of the harvest. Sif's story is intricately connected to her husband, Thor, the god of thunder, who embodies strength and protection. Together, they represent the balance between nurturing growth and defending it against chaos.

The Story of Sif and Loki's Mischief

One of the most well-known stories involving Sif centers around her golden hair and the trickster god Loki. According to the *Prose Edda*, Loki, known for his mischief and impulsive nature, cut off Sif's golden hair as a prank. This act enraged Thor, who threatened Loki with severe punishment. To atone for his actions, Loki promised to restore Sif's hair and enlisted the help of the dwarves, the master craftsmen of Norse mythology. The dwarves not only created new hair for Sif—imbued with magic that made it grow as naturally as her original locks—but also crafted other powerful artifacts, including Thor's hammer, Mjölnir.

The new hair, described as more radiant than the original, symbolizes renewal and the enduring nature of life. The story underscores themes of resilience and recovery, depicting Sif as a goddess whose strength lies in her ability to rebound from adversity. This tale reflects the cycles of the agricultural year, where even after hardship or loss, growth and prosperity can return with time and care.

Symbolic Connections: Wheat, Hair, and the Cycle of Growth

Sif's golden hair is a powerful symbol in Norse mythology, representing the fields of wheat and the bounty they provide. In an agrarian context, the cutting of Sif's hair can be seen as the harvest itself—a necessary action that, while appearing destructive, paves the way for new growth. The regrowth of her hair embodies the regenerative power of the earth and the promise of future harvests.

The tale of Sif's hair also emphasizes the importance of community and the divine interconnectedness that maintains balance in the world. Just as Loki's actions and the subsequent efforts to repair the damage involved the gods and dwarves alike, the agricultural process was a collective endeavor that required collaboration, preparation, and respect for the natural world.

Rituals and Agrarian Practices

Both Mokosh and Sif were central to the rituals and agricultural practices of their respective cultures. In Slavic tradition, festivals celebrating Mokosh included offerings of grain, bread, and milk, symbolizing the community's dependence on her blessings for rain and fertility. These rituals often took place near water sources or sacred groves, areas believed to be imbued with her presence.

In Norse culture, Sif's connection to the harvest was celebrated in the rituals surrounding the *blót*, a sacrificial ceremony where offerings were made to the gods to ensure prosperity and protection. The harvest festival, which marked the end of the growing season, was an occasion for feasting, storytelling, and honoring the gods with toasts and tributes. The symbolism of golden grain, present in stories of Sif's radiant hair, was often invoked in prayers and songs of gratitude for the harvest.

Poetic Passage: Hymn to the Harvest Goddesses

Mokosh, mother of earth and rain,
With spindle in hand, you ease our pain.
From seed to stalk, your blessings flow,
In fields you guard, green life does grow.

Sif, with hair of golden hue,
The wheat fields whisper, all for you.
Though cut and sheared, you rise anew,
In cycles bound, the old, the new.

Goddesses both, of land and light,
Your spirits guide us day and night.
In rituals deep, your names we sing,
To honor harvest's sacred ring.

Symbolic Connections Between Myth and Practice

The stories of Mokosh and Sif illuminate the deep-seated connection between mythology and agrarian life in Europe. Both goddesses embody the nurturing aspects of the earth, linking them to the essential practices of planting, harvesting, and renewal. This connection reflects the belief that divine influence was embedded in every seed sown and every stalk reaped, making the act of farming not just a practical task but a sacred one.

The rituals dedicated to these goddesses reinforced the idea that human beings were stewards of the earth, charged with maintaining harmony between the physical and spiritual worlds. The offerings made to Mokosh and the celebrations held in Sif's honor were acts of gratitude and reverence, reminding communities of their dependence on divine favor for survival and prosperity.

The Legacy of Mokosh and Sif in Modern Culture

Though times have changed, the influence of these goddesses can still be found in modern practices and cultural memory. In Slavic countries, the reverence for Mokosh has transitioned into traditions that celebrate the harvest, often with folk songs, dances, and rituals that echo ancient rites. Similarly, Sif's symbolism continues to inspire in Nordic culture, where harvest festivals and folklore remind communities of their deep connection to the land and its cycles.

These myths are also reflected in art, literature, and even contemporary pagan practices, where Mokosh and Sif are invoked as symbols of strength, fertility, and resilience. The stories of these goddesses remind us that the sacredness of the harvest and the reverence for the earth are timeless values, carried forward through generations and adapting to the evolving spiritual landscape.

Conclusion: The Sacred Ties Between Myth and Earth

The myths of Mokosh and Sif offer more than tales of goddesses; they encapsulate the fundamental relationship between human life and the land that sustains it. Through their stories, we see the embodiment of nurturing, sacrifice, and renewal that underpins agrarian life. Whether through the moisture and fertility of Mokosh or the radiant fields of Sif's golden hair, these goddesses symbolize the enduring bond between people and the natural world.

As we continue to explore harvest myths across cultures, the lessons imparted by Mokosh and Sif serve as a reminder of the shared human experience of reverence for the earth and the cycles that sustain life. Their legacies teach us that honoring the harvest means recognizing the interconnectedness of all life and the divine forces that guide it.

Chapter 7: The Wheat Mother of the Fertile Crescent

The Fertile Crescent, known as the cradle of civilization, stretches across parts of modern-day Iraq, Syria, Lebanon, Israel, and Egypt. It is within this rich and varied landscape that some of the earliest agricultural practices and myths about harvest deities were born. Chief among these goddesses is Inanna, the Sumerian goddess of fertility, love, and war, who holds a significant place in the mythology of the region. Her stories, intertwined with themes of life, death, and rebirth, resonate with the symbolic significance of wheat, which served as the foundation of sustenance and economic prosperity. This chapter will explore the myths of Inanna and the symbolic resonance of wheat, examining how these stories influenced agrarian practices and cultural beliefs in the ancient Middle East.

The Divine Attributes of Inanna: Goddess of Life and Renewal

Inanna, also known as Ishtar in later Akkadian traditions, was one of the most complex and revered deities in the Sumerian pantheon. She was depicted as a powerful and multifaceted goddess who governed fertility, sexual love, and warfare. Her domain extended from the heavens to the underworld, illustrating her role as a goddess capable of both nurturing life and invoking destruction. Inanna's connection to fertility linked her directly to the cycles of agriculture and the prosperity of her people.

The Story of Inanna's Descent

One of the most compelling myths surrounding Inanna is her descent into the underworld, a journey that symbolizes the cycle of life, death, and rebirth. According to Sumerian mythology, Inanna decided to visit her sister Ereshkigal, the queen of the underworld, to extend her influence beyond her usual realm. Before embarking on her journey, Inanna instructed her loyal servant, Ninshubur, to seek help from the gods if she did not return.

As Inanna descended through the seven gates of the underworld, she was required to remove a piece of her clothing or jewelry at each gate, symbolizing the gradual stripping away of power and worldly attachments. By the time she stood before Ereshkigal, she was naked and vulnerable. Ereshkigal, embodying the forces of death, sentenced her sister to death and hung her lifeless body on a hook. The earth above mourned Inanna's loss, resulting in the cessation of growth and a barren landscape—much like the fallow periods of agricultural cycles.

Ninshubur, following Inanna's instructions, sought assistance from the gods Enki and Enlil, who eventually intervened. With divine aid, Inanna was resurrected and allowed to return to the world of the living, bringing life and fertility back to the earth. Her resurrection marked the renewal of growth, symbolizing the return of abundance and the revival of agricultural productivity.

Poetic Passage: Inanna's Descent

Through gates of shadow, light's embrace,
The goddess walks with measured pace.
Jewels fall, like seeds in soil,
Power shed, through trial and toil.

Hung in darkness, lifeless, cold,
The earth above, a story told.
But whispers stir, and gods reply,
Inanna rises, death defied.

From barren ground, the wheat shall spring,
Life reclaimed, and harvest sing.

The Symbolism of Wheat: The Gift of the Gods

Wheat was a vital crop in the Fertile Crescent, sustaining life and becoming a symbol of prosperity, fertility, and divine favor. Its importance is seen in both practical and spiritual contexts, where the planting, growth, and harvesting of wheat mirrored the mythological themes of life, death, and resurrection. Inanna's descent and return from the underworld paralleled the planting of wheat seeds, which are buried in the earth only to rise and yield abundance.

The symbolism of wheat as a life-sustaining force is reflected in the numerous hymns and prayers dedicated to agricultural deities. Wheat was not merely a source of sustenance; it was considered a divine gift, representing the gods' benevolence and the perpetual promise of renewal. The annual cycle of sowing and reaping became a sacred act, imbued with rituals that acknowledged the interconnectedness of human effort and divine blessing.

The Rituals of Sowing and Harvest

In ancient Sumer, the act of planting wheat was a ritual in itself, performed with songs and offerings to ensure the favor of the gods. Farmers would invoke Inanna's blessing, recognizing her role as both the nurturer and the embodiment of resilience. The harvesting of wheat was similarly sacred, marked by festivals that included feasting, music, and ceremonies. These celebrations were meant to express gratitude for the goddess's return and the renewal she brought to the land.

Inanna's Dual Nature: Life and Death

The dual nature of Inanna, as both a bringer of life and a visitor to the underworld, reinforced the understanding that life and death were part of a continuous cycle. This duality reflected the agrarian reality of the ancient Middle Eastern world, where the sowing of seeds represented both an act of burial and an act of faith in their eventual resurrection as crops. The descent of the goddess into the underworld mirrored the seasonal decline of the land, while her return signified the rebirth of nature.

Inanna's complex nature as a goddess who transcends realms emphasized the balance between creation and destruction. This belief was integral to the spiritual practices of the time, as it acknowledged that growth could not exist without sacrifice, and that abundance was often the result of trials and transformations.

The Influence of Inanna on Agrarian Practices

The worship of Inanna had a profound impact on agrarian practices in the Fertile Crescent. Temples dedicated to her were often centers of agricultural planning, where priests and priestesses coordinated planting and harvest schedules, based on divine signs and celestial events. The temple grounds were sometimes used for communal storage of grain, ensuring that the bounty of the harvest was protected and shared among the people.

Offerings to Inanna, such as wheat, barley, and honey, were made as expressions of gratitude and requests for her continued favor. These offerings were believed to strengthen the connection between the divine and the earthly, reinforcing the sacred duty of humans to honor the gifts of the gods through responsible stewardship of the land.

Connections to Other Harvest Deities in the Region

The mythology of Inanna shares similarities with other harvest deities in the Middle East, such as the Canaanite goddess Anat and the Egyptian goddess Isis. Anat, like Inanna, was associated with fertility and war, embodying the duality of nurturing life and wielding power. Isis, known for her magical prowess and role as a mother figure, also symbolized renewal and resurrection, particularly through the story of her husband Osiris, whose death and rebirth influenced the flooding of the Nile and the subsequent renewal of the land.

These parallels highlight the widespread cultural understanding of fertility goddesses as both life-givers and agents of cyclical change. The symbolic connection between female deities and the growth cycles of crops underscored the belief that the feminine divine was essential for sustaining life and ensuring the continuity of prosperity.

Poetic Passage: The Wheat Mother's Song

Wheat mother, rise from earthen sleep,
From sacred soil, your promise keep.
Through rain and sun, the fields shall sway,
In golden dance, by light of day.

Inanna's breath, the harvest yields,
New life restored in fertile fields.
Beneath her gaze, the seeds are sown,
And from her gift, our bread is grown.

When seasons turn, and fields grow bare,
We look to you, our silent prayer.

For in your journey, we find our own,
Through loss and gain, we are not alone.

The Legacy of Wheat in Middle Eastern Culture

Wheat has remained a staple in Middle Eastern culture, not just as a food source but as a symbol of life and continuity. The myths surrounding deities like Inanna reinforced the sacredness of agriculture and the importance of maintaining harmony with the natural world. Even in contemporary times, harvest festivals and rituals that trace their origins to ancient practices continue to be celebrated in various forms, reflecting the enduring legacy of these beliefs.

The story of Inanna's descent, death, and rebirth serves as a timeless reminder of the resilience inherent in nature and humanity. Her myth embodies the lessons of patience, gratitude, and reverence for the cycles that sustain life. By understanding the symbolic resonance of wheat and the stories of the goddesses who protected it, we gain insight into how ancient cultures viewed the intricate dance between the divine, the earth, and human survival.

Conclusion: Inanna as the Eternal Wheat Mother

Inanna's place as the Wheat Mother of the Fertile Crescent symbolizes more than just the agricultural roots of a civilization; she represents the deep spiritual and practical connection between humans and the land they cultivate. Her mythology, rich with themes of sacrifice, renewal, and divine love, continues to speak to the universal human experience of growth, loss, and the promise of new beginnings.

As we move through the myths and traditions of various cultures, the story of Inanna remains a powerful example of how harvest goddesses embody not just fertility, but the profound cycles of life and death that sustain all of creation. Her legacy is one of resilience, teaching that even in the darkest moments of barrenness, the potential for renewal always exists, waiting to be awakened by the return of the divine.

Chapter 8: Pachamama: Earth Mother of the Andes

High in the vast, rugged landscapes of the Andes, where the mountains meet the sky, the people of the region have long revered Pachamama, the Earth Mother. As one of the most powerful and significant deities in Andean culture, Pachamama embodies fertility, abundance, and the nurturing spirit of the earth. Her influence is deeply embedded in agricultural practices, ceremonies, and the everyday lives of the Andean people. In this chapter, we will explore the mythology of Pachamama, her role in shaping agricultural customs, and how she is celebrated through rituals and festivals. Additionally, we will draw a comparative analysis with the Corn Mother, examining how these goddesses, though from different cultures, share universal themes of nurturing, sacrifice, and the cyclical nature of life.

The Mythology of Pachamama: The Sustainer of Life

Pachamama is more than a goddess; she is the personification of the earth itself, revered as both a protective and demanding force. Her name, derived from the Quechua words *pacha* (meaning earth, world, or time) and *mama* (meaning mother), signifies her all-encompassing presence as the mother of the land and all its resources. She is believed to be the provider of crops, livestock, and the fertility of the soil, ensuring that the cycle of life continues uninterrupted.

In Andean mythology, Pachamama is often depicted as a nurturing figure, with outstretched arms or holding fruits and grains that represent the bounty of the earth. However, she is also known for her dual nature. While she provides generously, she demands respect and care; if neglected or mistreated, Pachamama can cause natural disasters such as droughts, landslides, and earthquakes as a form of retribution. This belief underscores the reciprocal relationship between humans and nature, where harmony must be maintained to sustain life.

The Role of Pachamama in Agricultural Practices

Agriculture is the lifeblood of the Andean people, and Pachamama plays a central role in its success. The mountainous terrain and diverse climate of the Andes pose unique challenges to farming, making the blessings of Pachamama vital for a successful harvest. The traditional practice of *ayni*, or reciprocity, is fundamental to Andean agriculture and reflects the mutual care between humans and the Earth Mother. Farmers offer gratitude and gifts to Pachamama to ensure her continued favor and the fertility of the land.

Planting and Harvest Rituals

Planting and harvesting in the Andes are deeply spiritual acts, often accompanied by ceremonies dedicated to Pachamama. Before planting, farmers perform a ritual known as the *Pago a la Tierra* (Payment to the Earth), where offerings such as coca leaves, maize, chicha (a traditional fermented drink), and animal fat are buried in the ground as a symbolic act of gratitude. This ceremony is believed to feed Pachamama and show appreciation for her sustenance. By doing so, farmers hope to secure her blessing for abundant growth.

During harvest, another round of offerings and celebrations takes place to thank Pachamama for her generosity. These rituals are marked by music, dances, and communal feasting, reinforcing the social bonds within the community and the collective acknowledgment of the goddess's role in their survival.

Comparative Analysis: Pachamama and the Corn Mother

While Pachamama and the Corn Mother come from distinct cultural backgrounds—Andean and Native American respectively—they share notable similarities in their roles as embodiments of the earth and providers of life. Both deities represent the nurturing, feminine force that sustains human life through agriculture and natural abundance. However, there are also key differences that highlight the unique ways in which each culture interprets the relationship between humanity and the natural world.

Similarities

1. **Embodiments of the Earth**: Both Pachamama and the Corn Mother are revered as more than just deities; they are seen as personifications of the earth and its life-giving properties. They embody the concept of motherhood in a universal sense, providing nourishment and ensuring the continuity of life through their association with crops and fertility.

2. **Cycles of Life and Reciprocity**: The myths of both goddesses emphasize the cyclical nature of life, death, and renewal. Pachamama's demand for respect and offerings mirrors the Corn Mother's story of sacrifice, where she becomes the crops that sustain her people. In both cases, the relationship between humans and the goddess is one of mutual respect and reciprocity, highlighting the belief that taking from the earth must be balanced with acts of gratitude and care.

3. **Cultural Integration into Agricultural Practices**: Rituals involving Pachamama and the Corn Mother are integral to the planting and harvesting process. In Andean culture, offerings and prayers are made to Pachamama before sowing seeds, while Na-

tive American tribes may perform dances, songs, and ceremonies to honor the Corn Mother and ensure a fruitful season.

Differences

1. **Nature of Influence**: Pachamama's influence extends beyond agriculture to include the health of the environment as a whole. She is not only associated with fertility and crops but also with natural phenomena such as earthquakes and landslides, emphasizing her power over the stability of the land. In contrast, the Corn Mother's mythology focuses more narrowly on her role as the provider of maize and her sacrifice for the sake of her people's survival.

2. **Cultural Expression**: The rituals dedicated to Pachamama are communal and often involve elaborate ceremonies that include offerings of coca leaves, chicha, and animal sacrifices. These practices emphasize the collective nature of Andean society and its deep-rooted connection to the land. The Corn Mother, on the other hand, is often celebrated through storytelling, songs, and dances that convey her myth and the lessons of respect and gratitude for the harvest.

3. **Dual Nature and Retribution**: Pachamama is known for her dual nature as both a nurturing and punishing force. If disrespected or taken for granted, she may express her displeasure through natural disasters. The Corn Mother, while embodying sacrifice and transformation, does not exhibit the same retributive aspect. Her story is more focused on the themes of selflessness and renewal.

Symbolic Interpretations of Pachamama

Pachamama's symbolism extends far beyond her association with crops and fertility. She represents the interconnectedness of all life and the belief that humans are stewards of the earth. The offerings made to her symbolize not just gratitude but a reminder of humanity's role in maintaining the balance between consumption and conservation.

The Feminine Divine and Earth's Bounty

As a mother figure, Pachamama embodies the nurturing qualities of the feminine divine. She is the source from which life springs and the protector of all living beings. This maternal aspect aligns with the universal archetype of the Earth Mother found in various cultures, reinforcing the idea that the earth itself is alive and imbued with spirit. Pachamama's presence reminds the Andean people that they are her children, dependent on her gifts and responsible for treating her with care.

Reciprocity and Balance

The Andean concept of *ayni* reflects the belief that all actions must be reciprocated to maintain balance. This principle is evident in the rituals and practices dedicated to Pachamama. When farmers give offerings to the Earth Mother, they are not only asking for her favor but acknowledging their part in a greater cycle. This philosophy emphasizes the importance of living in harmony with nature and understanding that the earth's resources are finite and must be used responsibly.

Ceremonies and Festivals in Honor of Pachamama

The most significant time for honoring Pachamama is during the month of August, which marks the end of winter and the beginning of the agricultural year in the Andes. This period is considered the best time to make *Pago a la Tierra*, as the earth is believed to be hungrier and more willing to accept offerings. The ritual is performed by burying offerings such as coca leaves, maize, wine, and sweets in the ground while prayers and chants are recited.

During the annual *Fiesta de la Pachamama*, communities come together to celebrate with music, traditional dances, and shared meals.

The festivities serve as a reminder of the community's dependence on the Earth Mother and reinforce the values of unity and collective gratitude.

Poetic Passage: Pachamama's Embrace

In mountains high and valleys deep,
Where whispers of the ancients sleep,
Pachamama holds the earth,
Cradle of life, in endless birth.

Her arms spread wide, with fruits adorned,
A mother's touch, in sunlight warmed.
Yet fierce her gaze, if scorned or slighted,
Earth shall quake, her voice ignited.

Through seed and root, her spirit flows,
In every stalk, her blessing grows.
To her we sing, to her we give,
The breath of life, in which we live.

The Enduring Legacy of Pachamama

Pachamama's influence remains strong in contemporary Andean society, where traditional beliefs often coexist with modern practices. She is still invoked in agricultural rites, celebrated in festivals, and respected as a guardian of the land. The growing global awareness of environmental sustainability and the need for ecological balance has brought renewed interest in the teachings and values embodied by Pachamama.

Her story serves as a reminder that the earth is not just a resource to be exploited but a living entity that must be nurtured and respected. The principles of reciprocity, gratitude, and stewardship that underpin the worship of Pachamama are as relevant today as they were in ancient times.

Conclusion: The Universal Earth Mother

Pachamama's legacy as the Earth Mother of the Andes highlights the profound relationship between humans and the natural world. Her mythology, steeped in themes of fertility, reciprocity, and duality, teaches that the earth is both provider and protector. By drawing comparisons with the Corn Mother and other harvest deities, we see that the reverence for the nurturing feminine and the cycles of life is a shared human experience that transcends cultural boundaries.

As we continue to explore the myths of harvest goddesses, Pachamama's story reinforces the timeless truth that the earth is a sacred source of life, and maintaining balance with it is essential for survival and prosperity. The lessons from the Andes echo in the fields, forests, and traditions of people around the world, calling us to honor the earth and embrace our role as stewards of its abundant gifts.

Chapter 9: The Grain Maiden of Ancient Egypt

In the arid landscapes of ancient Egypt, where the Nile River breathed life into the land, the harvest was not only an economic necessity but a matter of survival. Central to this agricultural culture was Renenutet, the goddess of the harvest, fertility, and nourishment. Often depicted as a cobra or a woman with the head of a snake, Renenutet was revered as a divine protector of crops and a guarantor of abundance. Her presence and influence were essential for ensuring the prosperity of the fields and, by extension, the wealth and well-being of the people. This chapter will delve into the mythology surrounding Renenutet, her role in ancient Egyptian society, and her significance as a symbol of sustenance and fertility.

The Mythology of Renenutet: Guardian of the Harvest

Renenutet, whose name means "the one who nourishes," was considered a powerful deity associated with the fertility of the fields and the abundance of the harvest. She was often depicted in art as a serpent or a woman with a cobra's head, symbolizing her protective nature and connection to the fertility of the earth. In Egyptian mythology, the cobra was a powerful symbol of both protection and royalty, emphasizing Renenutet's status as a goddess who safeguarded the resources that sustained life.

Renenutet's role as a harvest deity extended to overseeing the growth and maturity of crops, particularly wheat and barley, which were staples in the Egyptian diet. The well-being of these crops was directly linked to the prosperity of the nation. It was believed that Renenutet's favor ensured that the grains would grow strong and plentiful, warding off pests, disease, and other threats that could decimate the harvest.

The Divine Role of Nourishment and Protection

Renenutet was not just a goddess of the fields but also a maternal figure who represented the nurturing aspects of the divine. Her association with nourishment extended beyond agriculture to the broader idea of divine care and providence. This aspect of her nature is reflected in her role as the protector of young children, whom she would shield with her maternal instincts and serpentine power.

Her nurturing presence was complemented by her dual nature as a goddess who could also be fierce and vengeful if disrespected. This duality reinforced the idea that while Renenutet was generous and protective, her favor was not to be taken for granted. Ancient Egyptians understood that their relationship with the goddess was based on respect and offerings, a principle that mirrored the delicate balance between human effort and divine intervention required for a successful harvest.

Poetic Passage: Renenutet's Watchful Eye

With scales that shimmer in the sun,
Renenutet, the steadfast one.
In fields of gold, she makes her home,
A guardian where grains are sown.
Her hiss commands both fear and awe,
The goddess rules by nature's law.
With gentle touch, she bids them rise,
Each stalk, a gift beneath her eyes.

The Role of Renenutet in Agricultural Practices

The Nile River's annual inundation was crucial for replenishing the soil with nutrient-rich silt, making the land fertile for planting. This cycle was a cornerstone of Egyptian agriculture and was intricately tied to the worship of gods who governed nature and fertility. Renenutet was one of the central figures in this divine hierarchy, believed to oversee the growth and maturation of crops once the waters receded and planting began.

Farmers would often conduct rituals and offer prayers to Renenutet before planting their seeds and during key stages of crop growth. These rituals were intended to invoke her blessing and ensure that the fields would thrive under her watchful protection. Offerings to Renenutet typically included food items such as milk, bread, and beer—products derived from the harvest she was believed to protect. These offerings were placed in small shrines or temple spaces dedicated to her, reinforcing the spiritual connection between the people, the land, and their deities.

The Harvest Festival: Celebrating Renenutet's Favor

One of the most significant times for honoring Renenutet was during the harvest festival, a period of communal celebration that marked the culmination of months of hard work. This festival, often held at the end of the harvesting season, was characterized by music, dancing, and feasting. It was a time for the community to come together and express gratitude for the goddess's favor and the abundance she had provided.

During the festival, farmers and priests would present offerings at her temples, and prayers of thanks would be recited. It was common for depictions of Renenutet in these temples to show her holding sheaves of wheat or surrounded by symbols of prosperity such as baskets of grain. These images served as a visual representation of her role as the provider of nourishment and the embodiment of fertility.

Renenutet's Symbolic Significance

Renenutet's iconography and symbolism reveal much about her significance in ancient Egyptian culture. The choice to depict her as a serpent speaks to her role as a guardian. The cobra was a powerful emblem of protection, often associated with the *uraeus*, the symbol worn by pharaohs as a mark of divine kingship. This connection highlights Renenutet's dual role as a protector of both the ruler and the agricultural heart of the nation.

The Snake as a Symbol of Regeneration

The snake, as a symbol, carried deep meanings of renewal and cyclical change in many cultures, and ancient Egypt was no exception. The shedding of a snake's skin represented rebirth and transformation, making the serpent an appropriate embodiment for a goddess of the harvest, whose cycles of growth, death, and renewal mirrored the life cycle of crops. Renenutet's form symbolized the regenerative power of the land, ensuring that life would continue through the seasons.

Comparative Analysis: Renenutet and the Corn Mother

Renenutet's story and significance can be compared with that of the Corn Mother from Native American mythology. While they emerge from different cultural contexts, both figures are central to their respective cultures' understanding of agriculture and the sacred nature of food production.

Similarities

1. **Goddesses of Fertility and Sustenance**: Both Renenutet and the Corn Mother embody the nurturing aspect of the earth and play pivotal roles in ensuring the fertility of the land. They are celebrated as providers of food and protectors of the harvest, with rituals and ceremonies dedicated to securing their favor.

2. **Symbolic Representation of the Harvest**: Renenutet's association with wheat and barley mirrors the Corn Mother's connection to maize. Both goddesses symbolize the staple crops that are essential for their people's survival and prosperity.

3. **Ritual Offerings**: Just as offerings are made to Renenutet, the Corn Mother is honored through songs, dances, and gifts, reinforcing the reciprocal relationship between humans and the divine in maintaining the cycles of growth and harvest.

Differences

1. **Dual Nature of Protection and Retribution**: Renenutet is known for her dual nature as a nurturing protector and a fearsome force capable of retribution. This aspect sets her apart from the Corn Mother, whose mythology focuses more on self-sacrifice and transformation rather than punishment.
2. **Broader Divine Role**: Renenutet's influence extends beyond just agriculture; she is also associated with nourishment in general, including protection of infants and ensuring prosperity. The Corn Mother's role, while deeply significant, is more narrowly focused on the life cycle of corn and the lessons of renewal and gratitude it represents.
3. **Iconography**: The visual depictions of Renenutet as a cobra or a woman with a cobra's head contrast with the Corn Mother's representation, which often depicts her as a human figure or embodied in the maize plant itself. These differences highlight the unique cultural expressions of divine femininity and protection in each mythology.

The Integration of Renenutet in Egyptian Society

Renenutet's presence was felt in many aspects of ancient Egyptian society, from the grand ceremonies conducted at temples to the personal shrines found in homes and fields. Her worship emphasized the importance of harmony with nature and recognition of the divine forces that governed life's essentials. Farmers viewed their relationship with her as a partnership, one that required both their labor and her blessing to yield the best results.

Her temples, often located in fertile regions or near granaries, served as centers for agricultural planning and distribution. Priests and priestesses dedicated to Renenutet would oversee rituals and advise farmers on the spiritual aspects of their work, blending practical knowledge with religious observance.

Poetic Passage: The Grain Maiden's Blessing

Lady of the fields, where grain takes flight,
In golden seas beneath the light.
Renenutet, hear our call,
Your watchful eye, our safeguard, all.

From furrowed earth to harvest's end,
Your spirit guides, your gifts you lend.
In offerings laid, in prayers deep,
We trust in you, our souls to keep.

Through sun and flood, through wind and fire,
Your power fuels the farmer's desire.
To plant, to reap, to sow again,
Renenutet, guardian of men.

Conclusion: Renenutet's Lasting Legacy

Renenutet's legacy as the Grain Maiden of ancient Egypt is a testament to the deep respect the Egyptians held for the forces that governed their survival. Her mythology and the rituals dedicated to her highlight the sacred connection between the divine and the earthly, emphasizing that human prosperity depends on maintaining balance with the natural world.

The goddess's dual nature as both a nurturing protector and a force to be revered speaks to the understanding that the earth's bounty is both a gift and a responsibility. The celebrations, prayers, and offerings to Renenutet were not just acts of devotion; they were expressions of gratitude and a reminder that the harvest, like life itself, is a cycle sustained by respect, effort, and the blessings of the divine.

In the broader context of harvest goddesses, Renenutet's story is a powerful example of how ancient cultures viewed agriculture as a sacred act, intertwined with myth, spirituality, and survival. Her tale reinforces the timeless lesson that nature must be cherished, protected, and honored, ensuring that the cycle of life continues to flourish.

Chapter 10: Shennong and the Five Grains

In the ancient heart of China, where civilizations flourished along the great rivers, agriculture became the cornerstone of society, shaping its culture, economy, and spiritual beliefs. Central to this development was the mythological figure Shennong, the Divine Farmer and one of the legendary Three Sovereigns who is credited with teaching humanity the vital art of agriculture and the knowledge of medicinal plants. Known as the God of Agriculture, Shennong is revered for his profound influence on the cultivation of crops and the introduction of the "Five Grains," which became essential staples for sustaining life. This chapter will explore Shennong's mythology, his contributions to the advancement of agricultural knowledge, and the cultural and symbolic significance of his story.

The Mythology of Shennong: The Divine Farmer

According to Chinese mythology, Shennong, whose name means "Divine Farmer" or "Divine Husbandman," was a benevolent and wise ruler who introduced the knowledge of farming and herbal medicine to early human society. He is often depicted as a man with the face of a human and the body of an ox or as a robust figure holding a plow, symbolizing his intimate connection to the land and its cultivation.

The legend states that Shennong was born with a transparent abdomen, allowing him to observe the effects of different plants as he consumed them. This miraculous trait enabled him to test thousands of herbs and plants, learning which were safe for consumption, which were poisonous, and which had medicinal properties. Through this arduous process, Shennong developed the foundational principles of Chinese herbal medicine, recorded in the ancient *Shennong Bencao Jing* (The Classic of Herbal Medicine).

Shennong's greatest gift to humanity, however, was the introduction of agriculture. Before Shennong's teachings, people relied on hunting and gathering, which provided an inconsistent food supply. The Divine Farmer showed them how to cultivate the land, grow crops, and establish a stable source of nourishment. The myth credits him with the discovery and promotion of the "Five Grains"—rice, millet, wheat, barley, and soybeans—which became the staples of Chinese agriculture and diet.

Poetic Passage: Shennong's Wisdom

From earth's embrace, a whisper came,
A god of soil, of plow, and flame.
Shennong, wise with gaze so clear,
Taught seeds to sprout and roots to steer.
With open chest, he bore the cost,
Of tasting leaf and finding loss.
Yet in his pain, he found the cure,
The grains of life, both rich and pure.
Fields of gold and harvests blessed,
Sprung forth from knowledge once confessed.

The Five Grains: Symbols of Life and Prosperity

The Five Grains (◇◇, *wǔgǔ*) hold deep symbolic significance in Chinese culture, representing sustenance, fertility, and the interconnectedness of life and nature. Each grain carried its own spiritual and practical meaning, essential for the nourishment and growth of society:

1. **Rice (◇, *dào*):** Revered as the most sacred of all crops, rice symbolizes life and prosperity. It was cultivated in the fertile, water-rich regions of southern China and became the foundation of traditional Chinese cuisine. Rice is often associated with abundance and is a symbol of wealth and nourishment.

2. **Millet (◇, *sù*):** Millet was one of the first grains to be domesticated in ancient China and holds significant historical importance. It is associated with endurance and resilience due to its ability to grow in arid conditions. Millet played a key role in sustaining life in the early agrarian communities of northern China.

3. **Wheat (◇, *mài*):** Wheat was introduced later and became a staple in northern China. It is associated with sustenance, prosperity, and the power to nourish the body and soul. Wheat also represents the communal effort needed for large-scale agriculture and food production.

4. **Barley (◇◇, *dàmài*):** Barley, known for its hardiness and adaptability, symbolizes strength and survival. It was often used in ancient rituals and was considered essential for producing food that could sustain a growing population.

5. **Soybeans (◇, *dòu*):** Soybeans are deeply rooted in Chinese culture, both as a food source and as a symbol of fertility and growth. Their high nutritional value made them a cornerstone of the Chinese diet, and they were often used in the creation of tofu and soy-based products. Soybeans embody nourishment and balance,

reflecting Shennong's emphasis on holistic health and the integration of nutrition into daily life.

Shennong's Contributions to Agricultural Practices

Shennong's impact on ancient agricultural practices was immense. By teaching the techniques of plowing, irrigation, and crop rotation, he helped establish farming as the primary means of subsistence for Chinese civilization. His lessons laid the groundwork for sustainable farming practices that promoted efficient land use and soil conservation.

Shennong's teachings emphasized the importance of working with the rhythms of nature. He encouraged farmers to observe the seasonal cycles, plant their seeds at the appropriate times, and follow the movements of the sun and moon to optimize their harvests. This harmony with the natural world became a core tenet of traditional Chinese agronomy and was reflected in the rituals and festivals that celebrated planting and harvest.

The Importance of Festivals and Rituals

Agricultural deities like Shennong were honored through various festivals and rituals that underscored the gratitude and reverence that the people felt for their harvests. The *Spring Festival* and other seasonal celebrations often included offerings of the Five Grains, dances, and songs that expressed appreciation for the abundance that Shennong's teachings provided. These rituals reinforced the spiritual belief that maintaining a respectful relationship with the earth and the deities that governed it was essential for continued prosperity.

The Symbolism of Shennong in Chinese Culture

Shennong's story carries profound symbolic meanings that extend beyond agriculture. His transparent abdomen, which allowed him to test herbs and determine their effects, symbolizes wisdom, sacrifice, and the pursuit of knowledge for the greater good. This trait underscores the belief that true leadership requires personal risk and a deep connection to one's people.

The Divine Farmer as a Model of Leadership

Shennong embodies the archetype of the wise ruler who serves his people selflessly. His contributions to agriculture and medicine illustrate the concept of *benevolent leadership*, where rulers are expected to provide not only governance but also practical knowledge that enhances the well-being of their subjects. This ideal became a model for subsequent rulers in Chinese history, who were often judged by their ability to support the agricultural needs of their populations and maintain harmony with nature.

The Interplay Between Health and Agriculture

Shennong's association with both agriculture and herbal medicine reflects the interconnectedness of diet, health, and overall well-being. This dual role emphasizes that food is not just a source of sustenance but a form of medicine, aligning with the Chinese principle that what one consumes plays a direct role in maintaining health and balance. This belief is foundational in traditional Chinese medicine, which continues to use plants and herbs discovered and classified during the mythological era of Shennong's teachings.

Shennong's Place Among the Three Sovereigns

Shennong is part of the legendary *Three Sovereigns* (三皇, *Sānhuáng*), mythical rulers who are said to have brought civilization to humanity. The other two members are Fuxi, the cultural hero credited with creating the trigrams of the *I Ching* and teaching fishing and hunting, and Nuwa, who is associated with creation and repairing the heavens. Together, the Three Sovereigns represent the foundational aspects of early human life: survival, society, and spirituality.

Shennong's role among the Three Sovereigns emphasizes his significance as the figure who taught people how to harness the land for sustenance. His contributions set the stage for China's agricultural development and the flourishing of early Chinese civilization.

Comparative Analysis: Shennong and Other Agricultural Deities

When comparing Shennong to other agricultural deities such as the Roman goddess Ceres or the Greek Demeter, certain similarities and differences emerge:

Similarities

1. **Teaching and Nourishing**: Like Ceres and Demeter, Shennong is revered for bringing knowledge of agriculture and food production to humanity. Each of these figures embodies the nurturing aspect of the divine, ensuring that people have the means to cultivate the land and sustain themselves.

2. **Symbolism of Fertility**: Shennong's association with the Five Grains parallels the grain symbols associated with Ceres and Demeter. All three deities represent fertility and abundance, reinforcing the idea that agriculture is a sacred gift from the divine.

Differences

1. **Dual Role in Medicine**: Unlike Ceres or Demeter, Shennong's contributions extend to the realm of herbal medicine. His role as both the god of agriculture and the father of Chinese medicine highlights the unique integration of food and health in Chinese culture, emphasizing the belief that nourishment is central to both physical and spiritual well-being.
2. **Cultural Integration**: Shennong's influence permeates not only agricultural practices but also traditional Chinese medicine and philosophy. His teachings laid the groundwork for holistic health practices, connecting the cultivation of the land with the cultivation of human health—a connection less emphasized in the mythologies of Ceres or Demeter.

Poetic Passage: The Song of the Divine Farmer
In fields of green, with steady hand,
Shennong walks the ancient land.
He sows the seeds of life and health,
A legacy of endless wealth.
With eyes that pierce both leaf and root,
He tastes the bitter, finds the fruit.
His sacrifice, a tale retold,
In grains of rice and harvests bold.
The Five Grains rise, in sun and rain,
A gift from one who bore the pain.
To him we bow, in feast and song,
Our thanks to Shennong, wise and strong.

The Legacy of Shennong

Shennong's legacy endures in the cultural and spiritual life of China. His contributions laid the foundation for agricultural practices that would sustain Chinese civilization for millennia. The importance of the Five Grains persists in modern Chinese culture, not just as food staples but as symbols of life, prosperity, and the enduring bond between humanity and the land.

In addition, Shennong's dual role as an agricultural and medicinal figure has left an indelible mark on traditional Chinese medicine, which continues to incorporate the principles of plant-based healing that he is said to have pioneered. His story reminds us that true wisdom lies in understanding the interconnectedness of life—how the earth's bounty nourishes the body and how knowledge, passed down through generations, nurtures the soul.

Conclusion: Shennong as a Cultural Pillar

Shennong stands as a testament to the profound respect and gratitude ancient China held for the earth and its gifts. His teachings on agriculture and herbal medicine highlight the belief that sustenance and health are divine blessings, made possible through harmony with nature and the diligent cultivation of the land. By introducing the Five Grains and pioneering the understanding of plant-based medicine, Shennong laid a foundation that would support Chinese civilization for centuries.

His story, with its themes of sacrifice, resilience, and wisdom, continues to inspire and remind us of the essential role that agriculture and stewardship of the land play in human life. Shennong, the Divine Farmer, remains a powerful symbol of nurturing leadership and the unbreakable bond between humanity and the natural world.

Chapter 11: Harvest Myths of West Africa

In the rich tapestry of West African mythology, deities and spirits play essential roles in guiding daily life and the cycles of nature. Among the pantheon of deities, Oshun, the Yoruba goddess of water, fertility, and love, stands out as a figure whose influence extends to the realms of agriculture and prosperity. The myths surrounding Oshun and her association with the nurturing of crops reveal a culture deeply connected to the land and dependent on the divine balance between humans and nature. This chapter will delve into the stories of Oshun and other harvest-related myths in West Africa, exploring their cultural significance and symbolic meanings, accompanied by poetic passages that capture the essence of these deities.

Oshun: The River Goddess of Fertility and Abundance

Oshun is one of the most venerated deities in the Yoruba pantheon, revered as the goddess of fresh water, fertility, love, and beauty. Her name is synonymous with vitality and growth, and she is often depicted as a beautiful woman adorned in golden attire, representing her association with wealth and prosperity. Oshun's connection to agriculture stems from her role as a provider of fresh water, a critical element for nurturing crops and sustaining life. Without her blessings, the land would remain parched, and the fields would fail to yield their bounty.

The Myth of Oshun's River and the Harvest

One popular myth tells of a time when the earth was barren and the Yoruba people faced a devastating drought. The rivers and streams had dried up, and the land was cracked and lifeless. Desperate, the people turned to the orishas (deities) for help, but none could remedy the situation. It was then that Oshun, with her unmatched grace and compassion, heard the cries of the people and decided to intervene.

Oshun, known for her affinity with rivers and freshwater, danced along the dry riverbeds, her golden skirts shimmering as she moved. With each step, her laughter rang out like a melody, and where her feet touched the earth, water began to trickle forth. The rivers swelled and surged, bringing life back to the parched land. Crops began to grow, and the people rejoiced as their fields turned green once more. Oshun's intervention was seen as an act of love and generosity, emphasizing her role as the life-giver and the source of abundance.

This story is celebrated in Yoruba culture as a reminder that Oshun's blessings must be honored to ensure continued prosperity. It also underscores the idea that water is sacred and that without it, life, growth, and fertility cannot exist.

Poetic Passage: Oshun's Dance of Renewal

Golden goddess, river's bride,
With steps that stir the rolling tide.
Fields once parched, now drink your song,
As rivers rise, both deep and strong.
From drought's despair to verdant feast,
Your laughter calls the harvest beast.
Oshun, queen of fertile lands,
With water's touch, life's law she commands.

The Symbolism of Water and Fertility

In West African cosmology, water is a powerful symbol of life, renewal, and spiritual cleansing. Oshun's connection to rivers highlights her role as a bridge between the physical and spiritual realms. Her influence ensures that life continues through the nourishment of crops, the fertility of the soil, and the growth of families. Water's essential role in agriculture reinforces Oshun's position as an agricultural deity whose presence is felt in every drop that sustains the earth.

The idea of fertility in West African myths goes beyond physical nourishment. It encompasses the spiritual well-being of the community and the harmonious relationship between humans and their environment. Oshun's stories teach that abundance is not merely a gift but a reciprocal relationship that requires respect, offerings, and communal rituals to maintain balance.

Rituals and Ceremonies in Honor of Oshun

Oshun is honored through various rituals and ceremonies that often involve offerings placed at riverbanks or sacred groves. These offerings may include honey, oranges, cinnamon, and gold items—each symbolizing different aspects of her power. Honey, in particular, is a sacred substance for Oshun, representing sweetness, love, and the promise of fertility and prosperity.

During the annual Oshun Festival in Osogbo, Nigeria, devotees gather to celebrate the goddess's blessings. The festival features processions to the Osun River, where priests and priestesses lead rituals and dances to honor the deity. Participants pray for fertility, health, and a bountiful harvest, reinforcing the belief that Oshun's favor is essential for the community's well-being.

Comparative Analysis: Oshun and Other Harvest Deities

Oshun's myths and the cultural practices surrounding her worship share similarities with other harvest deities around the world. The themes of fertility, water, and the nurturing aspects of the divine are common in many cultures.

Similarities

1. **Fertility and Abundance**: Like Demeter in Greek mythology or Ceres in Roman tradition, Oshun is associated with the cycles of growth and renewal. These goddesses are all revered as maternal figures who play critical roles in ensuring the fertility of the land and the prosperity of their people.

2. **Rituals and Offerings**: The practice of making offerings to secure the favor of a deity is a universal theme in agricultural societies. Just as offerings were made to Demeter for a successful harvest, the Yoruba people present gifts to Oshun to maintain her blessings and ensure the flow of water needed for crops.

3. **Water as a Symbol of Life**: Water's role as a life-giving force is evident in many cultures, from the Nile's significance in ancient Egypt to the sacred rivers of India. Oshun's connection to rivers

aligns with the global understanding of water as essential for agriculture and human survival.

Differences

1. **Elemental Association**: While Oshun is associated with water and its nourishing properties, other harvest deities may be more closely linked to the earth or specific crops. Demeter, for example, is directly associated with grain and wheat, while Oshun's influence spans fertility, love, and prosperity, embodied through the flowing rivers.
2. **Cultural Expression**: The ways in which these deities are honored can differ significantly. Oshun's rituals often involve dances, music, and offerings near water sources, emphasizing her joyous and loving nature. In contrast, some deities are honored through solemn rites that reflect the harshness of agricultural life or the bittersweet nature of their myths.

The Role of Other West African Deities in Agriculture

While Oshun is a prominent figure associated with water and fertility, other deities in West African mythology also play roles in the agricultural cycle. For example:

- **Orisha Oko**: The god of agriculture, Orisha Oko, is invoked for the health and productivity of the land. He represents the physical labor of farming and the prosperity that comes from diligent work. Offerings to Orisha Oko are meant to secure his protection against blights and ensure the growth of crops.
- **Yemoja**: Sometimes linked with Oshun, Yemoja is another water deity who is considered the mother of all orishas. Her influence on fertility extends to the sea and large bodies of water, symbolizing the deep, nurturing aspects of the divine feminine. She is celebrated for her role in nurturing life and promoting growth.

The Integration of Myth and Everyday Life

The myths of Oshun and other agricultural deities are more than stories; they are living elements of cultural identity that guide how people interact with the natural world. The reverence for water as a source of life, embodied by Oshun, informs practices of water conservation and communal respect for natural resources. The concept of abundance as a gift that must be honored with gratitude and care is central to the agricultural practices in many West African communities.

These beliefs are woven into the fabric of daily life, from planting and harvesting crops to the songs sung in the fields and the rituals performed at riverbanks. They serve as a reminder that the success of the harvest and the prosperity of the community depend not only on physical labor but on maintaining harmony with the spiritual forces that govern the land.

Poetic Passage: The Prayer to Oshun

Oshun, of the river's grace,
Golden light and gentle face.
We bring you gifts, in hopes you'll stay,
And bless our fields, our crops, our way.

With honey sweet and songs of praise,
We seek your laughter, your warming gaze.
O goddess kind, of fertile tide,
In you our hopes and dreams reside.

Let waters flow, let green seeds rise,
Beneath your watchful, loving eyes.
For in your name, we find our gain,
The harvest rich, the promised rain.

Conclusion: Oshun's Enduring Legacy

Oshun's role in West African mythology exemplifies the profound respect and gratitude that people have for the natural world and its cycles. As a goddess who embodies both the nurturing and joyous aspects of life, she represents the essence of fertility, love, and abundance. Her stories remind us that water is not only a physical necessity but a spiritual blessing, connecting human survival to divine favor.

The myths of Oshun and her counterparts continue to shape cultural practices, emphasizing the importance of balance, gratitude, and communal responsibility. By celebrating the stories and rituals dedicated to Oshun, the Yoruba people and other West African cultures maintain a connection to their heritage and the enduring belief that the earth's gifts must be cherished and respected.

As we explore the myths and deities associated with the harvest across different cultures, Oshun's tale serves as a beautiful reminder that abundance is not just harvested from the land but cultivated through relationships—with nature, the divine, and each other. Her legacy calls us to honor the interconnectedness of all life and to celebrate the cycles that sustain it.

Chapter 12: Tales from the Celtic Fields

The lush, green landscapes of Celtic regions were fertile grounds not only for crops but for the growth of rich mythology and folklore. Among these myths, deities and spirits related to the harvest played a crucial role in ensuring the cycles of life, death, and rebirth were honored and understood. Central to these tales are figures like Brigid, the goddess of fire, fertility, and agriculture, and the enigmatic Green Man, a symbol of nature's renewal and cyclical life. This chapter will explore these Celtic harvest myths, their significance, and the symbolic themes of rebirth and sacred rites embedded in these stories.

Brigid: The Goddess of Fire, Fertility, and the Harvest

Brigid, also known as Brigit or Brighid, holds a special place in Celtic mythology as a multifaceted deity associated with fire, fertility, healing, and poetry. She is revered as a goddess who bridges the practical and the mystical, embodying the nurturing and life-giving forces of nature. Brigid's influence spans agriculture and craftsmanship, making her an essential figure for communities that relied on the land and its bounties.

The Myth of Brigid and the First Harvest

One of the most enduring myths involving Brigid centers on the celebration of *Imbolc*, a festival held at the beginning of February to mark the halfway point between the winter solstice and the spring equinox. Imbolc is associated with the warming of the earth, the preparation of fields for planting, and the hope of new growth. As the goddess of fire, Brigid's flame was said to breathe life into the frozen land, encouraging the first signs of spring and heralding the coming of the planting season.

According to legend, Brigid would walk the fields with her staff, blessing the soil and ensuring that it would be fertile for the upcoming sowing. Farmers and families would light candles and bonfires in her honor, symbolizing the light she brought into the dark winter months. These flames were believed to carry her essence and invoke her favor for a prosperous planting season and an abundant harvest.

Brigid was also associated with healing and protection, making her an all-encompassing figure who represented the well-being of both the land and the people. She embodied the nurturing aspect of agriculture, where the earth, like a mother, must be cared for and respected to yield sustenance.

Poetic Passage: Brigid's Flame

O Brigid, queen of hearth and field,
Your flames ignite, our fates are sealed.
From frozen earth, your warmth does spread,
And stirs the seeds that once seemed dead.

With whispers soft, you coax the bloom,
Dispelling winter's shadowed gloom.
Through fire's light, the soil awakes,
And in your name, the harvest takes.

The Green Man: The Spirit of Nature and Renewal

The Green Man is a mysterious and iconic figure in Celtic mythology, symbolizing nature's eternal cycle of growth, death, and rebirth. He is often depicted as a face surrounded by or composed of leaves, branches, and vegetation, embodying the spirit of the forest and the power of regeneration. While not a harvest deity in the traditional sense, the Green Man's presence in myths and folklore is deeply connected to the agricultural cycle and the sacredness of nature.

The Symbolism of the Green Man

The Green Man represents the life force that animates all living things and the cyclical nature of existence. His leafy visage signifies the rebirth of plants and trees each spring after the dormancy of winter. This symbolism resonates with the concept of renewal found in agricultural practices, where the death of a crop is followed by the rebirth of a new planting season. The Green Man's face emerging from the greenery suggests the idea that nature itself has consciousness and that the earth is alive and capable of rejuvenation.

The Green Man is often associated with ancient rites and festivals that celebrate the coming of spring and the renewal of life. These rites would sometimes involve the weaving of plant and flower garlands, dancing, and rituals that invoked the spirit of nature to bless the fields and ensure the fertility of the land. The Green Man's image was often carved into churches and sacred sites, symbolizing humanity's reliance on and respect for the cycles of nature, even within a religious context.

The Connection to Harvest Rites

Although the Green Man is primarily associated with spring, his presence is also felt during the harvest season. In some myths, the Green Man's appearance in the fields signals the need to give back to the land after reaping its gifts. This concept of reciprocity is central to Celtic spirituality, where balance and harmony with nature are essential. Farmers would perform rituals and give offerings at the end of the harvest season, acknowledging that the land must be nourished and respected in preparation for the next cycle of growth.

Symbolic Themes of Rebirth and Sacred Rites

Both Brigid and the Green Man embody the themes of rebirth and sacred rites that are central to Celtic mythology and agricultural practices. These themes are reflected in the following ways:

The Cycle of Life and Renewal

The myths of Brigid and the Green Man highlight the cyclical nature of life. Brigid's flame and the warming of the earth during *Imbolc* symbolize the return of life and light after the cold, dark winter. Similarly, the Green Man's leafy face represents the annual rebirth of nature, where each spring marks the renewal of vitality in the fields, forests, and human communities.

These themes remind us that death is not an end but a necessary part of life's cycle. The harvest, while marking the end of a growing season, is also the beginning of preparation for the next one. The stories of Brigid and the Green Man teach that with each end comes a new beginning, a lesson that reinforces hope and resilience.

Sacred Rites and Offerings

Celtic harvest rituals often included offerings and sacrifices to deities and nature spirits as acts of gratitude and reciprocity. These rites were more than just religious observances; they were integral to the community's connection with the natural world. Brigid's festivals featured bonfires, candle lighting, and the making of *Brigid's crosses* from rushes or straw, symbolizing her protection and blessings. The Green Man was celebrated through May Day and Beltane festivities, which involved dancing around the maypole and other rites of fertility and renewal.

These practices highlighted the belief that the land was sacred and that the harvest was a divine gift. By performing rituals and honoring the deities and spirits that governed nature, the Celtic people maintained a spiritual bond with the earth that supported them.

Comparative Analysis: Brigid, the Green Man, and Other Harvest Deities

When comparing Brigid and the Green Man to other harvest deities, several commonalities and distinctions emerge:

Similarities

1. **Embodiment of Nature's Cycles**: Like Demeter, Ceres, and Oshun, Brigid and the Green Man embody the cycles of life, death, and rebirth. Their myths emphasize the idea that life is a continuous loop, where endings lead to new beginnings.

2. **Symbolic Rituals**: Harvest deities often inspire rituals and ceremonies that reinforce communal and spiritual ties. The bonfires of *Imbolc* and the offerings to the Green Man share similarities with other cultural practices that celebrate planting and harvest times.

3. **Nurturing and Protective Qualities**: Brigid's role as a protective goddess and the Green Man's representation of nature's growth align with the nurturing aspects seen in deities like Renenutet and Pachamama. These figures all protect and sustain

human life through their association with fertility and the natural world.

Differences

1. **Elemental Associations**: Brigid's connection to fire sets her apart from other agricultural deities who are more closely tied to earth or water. This elemental link emphasizes her role in transformation and rejuvenation, both of the land and the spirit.
2. **The Green Man's Ambiguity**: Unlike more clearly defined harvest deities, the Green Man is a more abstract figure, representing the life force of nature rather than specific agricultural practices. His symbolism is less about direct intervention and more about embodying the essence of natural cycles.
3. **Cultural Integration**: Brigid was both a goddess and, later, a Christianized saint, showing how Celtic pagan traditions were woven into Christian practices. The Green Man, carved into churches and sacred sites, reflects how Celtic reverence for nature was subtly preserved even as religious practices evolved.

Poetic Passage: The Green Man's Song
In the shadows, leaves entwined,
A face appears, both old and kind.
With eyes that know the woods' deep lore,
The Green Man wakes, as springs restore.
He whispers secrets to the trees,
And stirs the fields with every breeze.
When crops are reaped, his spirit sighs,
A promise kept beneath the skies.
In golden sheaf and harvest gold,
His tales of life and death are told.
And when the chill of winter falls,
The Green Man waits, as silence calls.

The Integration of Myth and Daily Life

For the Celtic people, myths were not just stories but frameworks through which they understood their place in the world. The presence of Brigid in everyday life was felt in the hearth fires that warmed homes and the rituals performed to bless the fields. The Green Man's image in architecture and art served as a reminder of the sacredness of nature and the cycles that governed human existence.

These myths reinforced the belief that humans were part of a larger system that required respect, reciprocity, and celebration. By weaving tales of Brigid and the Green Man into the fabric of daily life, the Celts maintained a cultural and spiritual bond with the land, ensuring that each harvest was not only a physical act of gathering food but a sacred rite that honored life itself.

Conclusion: The Sacred Cycles of the Celtic Fields

The tales of Brigid and the Green Man offer profound insights into the Celtic understanding of the harvest and the natural world. These figures embody themes of rebirth, resilience, and the sacred rites that link humanity to the earth. Brigid's flame represents the warmth and hope that carry communities through the cold months, while the Green Man's leafy visage reminds us of nature's capacity for renewal and the promise of spring.

As we explore the myths of other cultures, the stories from the Celtic fields stand as testament to the universal belief that life is cyclical, and that each harvest is both an end and a beginning. These tales call us to honor the land, recognize our place within the cycles of nature, and celebrate the gifts that sustain us. The legacy of Brigid and the Green Man continues to inspire, urging us to keep the sacred connection between humans and the earth alive in our modern world.

Chapter 13: The Sacred Corn of the Maya

For the ancient Maya, maize was not just a crop; it was the essence of life itself. It played an integral role in their mythology, sustenance, and identity, making the Maize God one of the most revered figures in their pantheon. The myths surrounding the Maize God, found in ancient texts and depicted in carvings and artifacts, reveal a deep spiritual connection between the Maya people and the crop that sustained them. This chapter delves into the detailed storytelling of the Maize God, its cultural and religious significance, and the interpretations of ancient Mayan texts and carvings that highlight this sacred relationship.

The Myth of the Maize God: The Source of Life

The Mayan Maize God, known as *Hun Hunahpu* or simply the Maize God, is at the center of the creation myths that explain humanity's origins. According to these myths, the gods attempted to create humans multiple times, using different materials. The first attempts, made from mud and wood, failed as these beings lacked understanding, emotion, and the capacity for worship. Finally, the gods created humans from maize dough, which became the successful creation that could think, feel, and express gratitude to the gods.

This myth signifies the importance of maize as the very fabric of human existence in Mayan culture. The Maize God himself symbolizes fertility, rebirth, and the cycle of life and death that mirrors the planting and harvesting of corn.

The Journey of the Maize God

One of the most profound stories involving the Maize God is his journey through the underworld, *Xibalba*, and his subsequent rebirth. This narrative is a testament to the Mayan belief in the cyclical nature of life and the idea that death is not an end but a transition. The Popol Vuh, the sacred text of the K'iche' Maya, recounts how the Maize God was sacrificed by the lords of the underworld and buried. From his body, maize sprouted, symbolizing rebirth and the promise of sustenance.

The myth continues with the twin sons of the Maize God, *Hunahpu* and *Xbalanque*, who venture into the underworld to avenge their father. Their victory over the lords of Xibalba ensures the Maize God's resurrection, an event that heralds the renewal of life and fertility on earth. This story, with its themes of sacrifice, struggle, and rebirth, is a powerful metaphor for the agricultural cycle. The planting of maize involves burying the seed in the ground, a symbolic death, followed by the seed's emergence as a plant—a resurrection.

Poetic Passage: The Maize God's Rebirth

In the depths of Xibalba's night,
A seed was sown, out of sight.
Hun Hunahpu, cut and laid,
Became the grain from which life's made.

Twin sons rise, brave and true,
Through trials deep, they break through.
From dark to light, from death to green,
The Maize God wakes, renewed, unseen.

Golden stalks, with sun's embrace,
Feed the people, time and space.
For in his tale, we learn and know,
Life returns where corn does grow.

The Cultural Significance of the Maize God

The Maize God's significance extends beyond mythology and into the daily lives of the Maya. Maize was more than a staple crop; it was a sacred substance intertwined with social, economic, and religious practices. The reverence for the Maize God was evident in the agricultural rituals performed throughout the year to ensure a successful planting and harvest.

Rituals and Offerings

Mayan rituals dedicated to the Maize God involved offerings of maize, cacao, and other crops, as well as dances, songs, and prayers. These rituals were often conducted by priests or shamans who acted as intermediaries between the people and the gods. The ceremonies emphasized the reciprocity between humans and the divine; the gods provided maize, and the people offered gratitude and devotion in return.

One significant ritual was the *sac ha'*, or the pouring of a maize-based drink as an offering to the gods. This act symbolized the pouring of life and the acknowledgment that the sustenance provided by the Maize God was vital for the community's survival. The liquid offerings were often mixed with other sacred substances like honey and chocolate, amplifying the ritual's importance and sacred nature.

Interpretation of Ancient Texts and Carvings

The reverence for the Maize God is preserved in Mayan texts such as the Popol Vuh and depicted in carvings found at archaeological sites like Palenque and Copan. These carvings portray the Maize God as a youthful, handsome figure with an elongated head, a characteristic shape that mimics an ear of corn. He is often shown surrounded by maize plants or with his hair styled to resemble maize tassels, emphasizing his identity as the life-giving deity.

In the Temple of the Inscriptions at Palenque, carvings depict scenes of the Maize God's journey through the underworld and his eventual resurrection. These artistic representations served as a reminder of the Maize God's power and the sacred nature of maize itself. The iconography reflects the deep-rooted belief that human life and maize are intertwined, each dependent on the other.

Symbolic Analysis of Carvings

The carvings and murals of the Maize God are rich with symbolism. The depiction of maize plants growing from the god's body suggests that life arises from death, an idea that reinforces the agricultural cycle and the concept of rebirth. The presence of water motifs alongside the Maize God indicates the essential role of rain in nurturing crops, symbolizing the interconnectedness of natural elements and the divine.

The symbology in these carvings also underscores the Mayan understanding of the universe as an interconnected whole. The Maize God's death and resurrection were not just personal to the deity but reflected cosmic principles of creation and renewal. The portrayal of maize as growing from the god's body links the divine to the physical world, illustrating that sustenance is a sacred gift from the gods, cultivated with human effort and divine blessing.

The Maize God and Modern Mayan Culture

The legacy of the Maize God endures in modern Mayan culture, where maize continues to be a staple food and a symbol of life. Festivals and rituals that honor the planting and harvesting of maize are still performed, preserving the connection to the ancient myths and their teachings. The importance of maize is reflected in traditional dishes like *tortillas*, *tamales*, and *atole*, which remain central to the diet and hold cultural significance.

Modern Mayan communities often integrate traditional beliefs with contemporary religious practices, blending Catholicism with indigenous rituals that honor the Maize God and other deities. This synthesis preserves the spiritual heritage of the Mayan people and maintains their bond with the land and its cycles.

Comparative Analysis: The Maize God and Other Agricultural Deities

When comparing the Mayan Maize God to other agricultural deities, certain similarities and differences emerge:

Similarities

1. **Rebirth and Renewal**: The story of the Maize God's death and resurrection mirrors the myths of Demeter and Persephone in Greek mythology and the rebirth themes found in the stories of deities like Osiris in Egyptian mythology. All these myths emphasize the cyclical nature of life and the idea that death is a necessary precursor to new life.

2. **Central Role in Culture**: Like other agricultural deities such as Ceres and Pachamama, the Maize God was central to the identity and survival of the people. His story was not just a tale but a framework for understanding the cycles of planting, growth, and harvest.

3. **Sacred Rites and Offerings**: The rituals performed in honor of the Maize God, involving offerings and prayers, are similar to those dedicated to agricultural deities in other cultures. The act of making offerings to secure a bountiful harvest is a universal theme in agrarian societies.

Differences

1. **Integration with Creation Myths**: The Maize God's role in the creation of humans from maize is unique to Mayan culture. While other cultures have myths of creation involving clay, water, or divine breath, the Maya specifically linked human existence to maize, reinforcing the sacred nature of the crop.
2. **Journey Through the Underworld**: The detailed journey of the Maize God through Xibalba and his connection to the Hero Twins adds a layer of narrative complexity not seen in all agricultural myths. This journey emphasizes not only the agricultural cycle but the cosmic struggle between life and death, good and evil.
3. **Artistic Representation**: The visual depiction of the Maize God as a young figure with corn-like features is distinctive. While many cultures personify their deities in human or partially human forms, the Maize God's unique portrayal emphasizes his direct connection to the crop itself.

Poetic Passage: The Gift of Maize

From gods above, a gift was made,
In golden husks, creation laid.
The Maize God's flesh, the earth's delight,
Sown in darkness, brought to light.

With rain and sun, with blood and sweat,
We honor him, we pay our debt.
For every stalk that bends and sways,
Carries whispers of ancient days.

Through fields we walk, through seasons' turn,
In each green blade, his lessons burn.
Life, like maize, is born, then dies,
Only to rise with hopeful cries.

Conclusion: The Eternal Corn

The story of the Maize God encapsulates the essence of Mayan spirituality, emphasizing the interconnectedness of life, death, and rebirth. His myth is a testament to the belief that maize is not just a crop but a divine gift that sustains life and represents the cycle of existence. The reverence for the Maize God, evident in ancient texts, carvings, and modern practices, highlights the deep cultural significance of maize as the lifeblood of the Maya.

As we explore the myths and agricultural deities of other cultures, the tale of the Maize God stands out for its profound integration into the identity and survival of an entire civilization. His story reminds us that sustenance is sacred, rooted in divine generosity and human resilience. The Maize God's legacy calls us to respect the natural cycles that nourish life and to honor the deep connection between humanity and the land that feeds it.

Chapter 14: The Symbolism of Seeds and Harvest

Throughout the ages, seeds and the act of harvesting have been powerful symbols interwoven into myths, spiritual practices, and cultural traditions across the world. Seeds carry potent metaphorical meaning, representing potential, life, death, and rebirth. The process of planting seeds and harvesting crops transcends mere agricultural practice—it is imbued with layers of symbolism that speak to human existence, the cycles of nature, and the divine connection between humanity and the earth. This chapter will delve into the themes of seeds and harvest as seen through various cultural myths and legends, weaving in poetic expressions and metaphors that encapsulate their rich meanings.

Seeds as Symbols of Potential and Creation

The seed, in its simplest form, embodies the essence of potential. A tiny, seemingly insignificant object, it contains within it the blueprint for growth, transformation, and new life. Across different mythologies, seeds are portrayed as the beginning of creation, the source from which all life springs.

The Creation Myths

In many cultures, the act of creation is likened to the planting of a seed. For example, in the Hindu tradition, the universe is said to have originated from a cosmic seed, known as the *Brahmanda* or "cosmic egg." This seed contained the potential for all creation and, when it burst open, released the cosmos in all its complexity. Similarly, in Greek mythology, Gaia, the earth mother, was believed to have brought forth life from the seeds she nurtured within her fertile body.

The ancient Egyptians also revered seeds as symbols of rebirth. The story of Osiris, the god of the afterlife and vegetation, highlights the cycle of death and renewal. After Osiris's body was dismembered and scattered, his wife, Isis, collected his parts and, with her magic, restored him to life. From his body, crops and grains grew, symbolizing that death is not an end but a gateway to new life. This myth underscores the belief that seeds, like Osiris, must be buried (a symbolic death) before they can sprout and renew the earth.

Poetic Passage: The Seed's Promise

Small and silent, held in hand,
A seed's potential, vast and grand.
Within its shell, a hidden power,
Awaits the rain, the sun, the hour.

Buried deep, in dark embrace,
It finds its strength, begins its race.
From death it stirs, from soil it wakes,
A tender shoot, the earth it breaks.

Life reborn, from husk to green,
The promise kept, the dream unseen.

Planting as a Metaphor for Hope and Labor

Planting seeds is an act steeped in hope and commitment. It requires labor, patience, and trust in the unseen forces of nature. Across cultures, myths involving planting symbolize the toil and faith needed to nurture growth, whether literal or metaphorical.

The Story of Demeter and Persephone

The Greek myth of Demeter and Persephone provides a powerful example of planting as a symbol of hope and resilience. When Persephone was taken to the underworld by Hades, her mother, Demeter, goddess of agriculture, mourned her loss, causing the earth to become barren. It was only through Persephone's return that Demeter's grief was eased and the earth could bloom once more, bringing forth crops and flowers. This myth is an allegory for the sowing of seeds in the dark soil (Persephone's descent) and the eventual growth and harvest (her return), encapsulating the hope that spring and new life will always come after the cold and death of winter.

In this context, planting is more than an agricultural act—it is an expression of faith that the future holds renewal and growth. The labor involved in planting becomes a sacred act, acknowledging the cycles of loss and recovery inherent in both nature and human life.

The Significance of Ritual Planting

In many indigenous cultures, planting seeds is accompanied by rituals and prayers that invoke divine blessings. The Mayan people, for instance, performed ceremonies that honored the Maize God, expressing gratitude and asking for a bountiful harvest. These rituals reinforced the idea that planting was a sacred partnership between humans and the divine, a reminder that nature's gifts were both a privilege and a responsibility.

The Harvest as a Symbol of Fulfillment and Gratitude

The act of harvesting represents the culmination of labor and the realization of potential. It is celebrated across cultures as a time of abundance, gratitude, and reflection on the cycles of life. Harvest myths often feature themes of divine favor, communal celebration, and the sharing of resources.

The Tale of Ceres

The Roman goddess Ceres, whose Greek counterpart is Demeter, was revered as the protector of agriculture and the provider of grain. The word "cereal" is derived from her name, highlighting her association with nourishment. In Roman culture, the *Cerealia* festival was held in her honor, featuring rituals, games, and sacrifices to give thanks for the harvest. This celebration acknowledged that the success of the harvest was due to both human effort and the goddess's blessings. The harvest, in this sense, is not just the end of a season but a sacred time to reflect on the divine and human partnership that made abundance possible.

The Symbol of the Harvest Feast

The harvest feast is a powerful symbol found in many cultures, representing gratitude, community, and the sharing of abundance. In West African traditions, festivals honoring deities like Oshun and Orisha Oko include communal feasts that celebrate the prosperity of the land.

These gatherings are moments of joy, dance, and music, reinforcing social bonds and collective thanksgiving.

Harvest celebrations also remind communities of the cyclical nature of life. The fruits of labor are enjoyed, but they also mark the beginning of the next cycle of sowing and growth. This continuity is reflected in myths that highlight the importance of balance and reciprocity in human relationships with the land and the divine.

Seeds and Harvest in Sacred Texts and Carvings

Ancient texts and carvings often capture the symbolism of seeds and harvests as metaphors for life's deeper meanings. In Mayan culture, for example, the Popol Vuh describes how humans were created from maize dough, linking human life to the sacred crop. Carvings of the Maize God show him adorned with maize stalks, emphasizing his role as the provider and protector of the harvest. These artistic depictions serve as a visual reminder that the cycle of planting and reaping is a reflection of life itself—a journey from potential to fulfillment and back to potential.

Similarly, Egyptian carvings of Osiris show him with stalks of wheat or emerging from the earth, signifying the resurrection that follows death. These images reinforce the understanding that the harvest is not just a gathering of crops but a moment that encapsulates the promise of life renewed.

Poetic Passage: The Harvest's Song

From toil and sweat, the harvest grows,
A gift from earth, in sun's warm glows.
Hands that planted, hearts that prayed,
Reap the bounty, efforts repaid.

Golden grain and fruits of vine,
Bless the table, feast and wine.
In laughter shared and stories told,
We honor cycles, ancient, old.

Yet as we taste this year's sweet yield,
We turn again, to furrowed field.

For life's a wheel, round and round,
In seed and harvest, sacred bound.

The Cycle of Death and Rebirth

Central to the symbolism of seeds and harvest is the theme of death and rebirth. The act of planting involves burying a seed, a symbolic death, which then transforms into a living plant. This process mirrors myths of deities who undergo death only to rise again, such as Osiris, the Maize God, and Persephone. These stories emphasize that death is a necessary part of the cycle of life, a precursor to growth and renewal.

This theme is especially evident in the Christian tradition, where the death and resurrection of Jesus Christ are compared to the sowing and harvesting of grain. The parable of the grain of wheat, found in the Gospel of John, states: "Unless a grain of wheat falls into the earth and dies, it remains alone; but if it dies, it bears much fruit." This metaphor reflects the idea that sacrifice and surrender can lead to greater abundance and life.

The Spiritual Lessons of Seeds and Harvest

The myths and symbols of seeds and harvest teach several profound spiritual lessons:

1. **Patience and Trust**: Planting a seed requires trust that it will grow, even when buried in darkness. This symbolizes faith in unseen processes and the patience to await results.

2. **Effort and Reciprocity**: The harvest is a reward for labor, but it also teaches the importance of giving back to the earth and expressing gratitude. Offerings and rituals underscore the belief that abundance comes from mutual respect between humanity and the divine.

3. **Cycles of Renewal**: The cycle of planting and reaping reflects life's natural rhythms—birth, growth, death, and rebirth. It is a reminder that endings are not final but part of an eternal cycle of renewal.

Conclusion: The Eternal Dance of Seeds and Harvest

The symbolism of seeds and harvest is deeply embedded in myths, sacred texts, and cultural practices around the world. These elements embody themes of potential, labor, hope, gratitude, and renewal. The planting of a seed and the gathering of the harvest are more than agricultural acts; they are sacred rituals that mirror the cycles of life and the journey of the human spirit.

From the myths of the Mayan Maize God to the stories of Demeter, Osiris, and the Green Man, the themes of seeds and harvest serve as reminders that life is a continuous cycle. Each seed holds the promise of new life, each harvest is a moment of fulfillment, and each death paves the way for rebirth. These universal lessons connect us to the earth, to the divine, and to each other, highlighting the sacredness of growth and the eternal dance of life.

Chapter 15: Legends of Sacrifice and Renewal

The theme of sacrifice as a precursor to abundance is woven into the mythologies of many cultures around the world. These stories often illustrate that the act of giving something precious—whether life, labor, or offerings—paves the way for growth, fertility, and renewal. The Aztec tales of Xilonen, the goddess of young maize, stand as powerful examples of this motif. In these stories, sacrifice is not just a ritual but a cosmic necessity that sustains life and ensures the continuity of nature's cycles. This chapter will explore myths involving sacrificial acts that lead to harvest abundance, with a focus on the Aztec legends of Xilonen, and discuss the symbolic meanings of life cycles and renewal inherent in these stories.

The Aztec Goddess Xilonen: The Maiden of Maize

Xilonen, known as the goddess of tender or young maize, is a prominent figure in Aztec mythology. She embodies the life-giving properties of maize, which was central to the sustenance and culture of the Aztec people. Her name means "the Hairy One," referencing the tassels of corn silk that crown the maize plant, symbolizing the goddess's connection to growth and fertility.

Xilonen's role in Aztec society was more than symbolic; she was central to agricultural rituals and ceremonies that honored the gods and ensured the prosperity of the crops. These rituals often involved acts of sacrifice, which were seen as essential to appeasing the gods and maintaining the balance between life and death. The Aztecs believed that life was sustained through offerings to the divine, a belief that was deeply embedded in their worldview.

The Festival of Xilonen

One of the most significant celebrations dedicated to Xilonen was the *Huey Tozoztli*, a festival held in her honor during the time when young maize began to ripen. The festival included feasting, dances, and ritual sacrifices, all aimed at securing the goddess's blessings for a plentiful harvest. The sacrificial ceremonies were elaborate and involved offerings of flowers, food, and, in some cases, human life. The sacrificial victims, chosen for their purity and strength, were seen as embodiments of the gods and were believed to join them in the afterlife as honored spirits.

This ritual sacrifice was not viewed with horror but with reverence. The Aztecs believed that the gods themselves had sacrificed their own blood to create and sustain humanity. Therefore, human sacrifice was seen as a reciprocation of that divine gift, ensuring that the cycle of life would continue. The sacrifice of life for the promise of abundance exemplified the belief that renewal comes only through the giving of oneself, echoing the cycles of nature where seeds must die in the soil to sprout and yield new life.

Poetic Passage: The Offering

The drums do sound, the people sing,
For Xilonen's breath, for harvest's spring.
With maize's crown and flowers' bloom,
We dance to ward away the gloom.

An offering, pure, for earth to take,
A gift of life, for life's own sake.
In shadow's death, the green shall rise,
Renewal's promise, beneath the skies.

Oh, maiden fair, of golden hue,
We give to you, you give anew.

Symbolic Meaning of Sacrifice in Aztec Culture

In Aztec cosmology, sacrifice was deeply connected to the concept of *tonalli*, a vital force that existed in both gods and humans. The act of sacrifice released this sacred energy, feeding the gods and empowering them to continue their divine work of sustaining the universe. This understanding of sacrifice highlights a profound sense of reciprocity: humans give to the gods so that the gods may give back in the form of rain, fertility, and the growth of crops.

Xilonen's myth, along with the rituals dedicated to her, symbolized the belief that life is cyclic and that each ending is a precursor to a new beginning. This is mirrored in the life cycle of maize, which must be planted and buried in the soil—symbolically dying—before it can grow and be harvested. The sacrifice of the individual for the greater good underscored the collective identity of the Aztec people, emphasizing that personal sacrifice was part of the natural order that maintained societal and cosmic harmony.

Myths of Sacrifice and Renewal in Other Cultures

The theme of sacrifice leading to renewal is not unique to Aztec mythology. Many cultures have similar tales where a god, goddess, or mythical figure sacrifices themselves or undergoes suffering for the benefit of the community or the natural world. These stories reinforce the idea that death is a necessary step toward rebirth and that abundance comes from acts of giving.

The Tale of Demeter and Persephone

In Greek mythology, the story of Demeter and Persephone offers a different, yet related, perspective on sacrifice and renewal. Persephone, the daughter of Demeter, is taken to the underworld by Hades, causing Demeter to mourn and withdraw her nurturing influence from the earth. The resulting barren landscape represents the symbolic death of nature. Persephone's eventual return to the surface, albeit for only part of the year, allows the earth to bloom again. This story highlights the idea that sacrifice and suffering—Demeter's grief—are necessary for the cycle of growth and renewal to continue.

Unlike the Aztec belief in literal sacrifice, the Greek myth focuses on emotional and seasonal sacrifice. The cyclical departure and return of Persephone symbolize the planting of seeds (burial and dormancy) and the growth that follows when conditions are right. This tale reinforces the belief that life is cyclical, governed by periods of loss and rebirth.

The Sumerian Myth of Inanna

Inanna, the Sumerian goddess of love, fertility, and war, undergoes a sacrificial journey to the underworld, where she must relinquish her garments and symbols of power at each of the seven gates. Once she reaches the realm of her sister, Ereshkigal, Inanna is stripped of everything and ultimately killed. However, through divine intervention and the lament of the gods, she is revived and allowed to return to the world above. Inanna's descent and resurrection symbolize the death of crops during harsh seasons and their regrowth in spring, illustrating the eternal cycle of sacrifice and renewal.

This myth shares thematic elements with the Aztec tale of Xilonen, where the willingness to undergo suffering or death leads to the rejuvenation of life. The descent into darkness is seen as a transformative phase that must occur before the return of life and prosperity.

The Cultural Lessons of Sacrifice and Harvest

The legends of sacrifice and renewal found in cultures around the world share common themes and lessons that continue to resonate. These stories emphasize that abundance and prosperity are not gifts taken for granted; they require dedication, labor, and sometimes great sacrifice. The myths teach that there is value in hardship, as it prepares the ground for future growth and ensures that the cycles of life and nature continue.

Life Cycles and the Role of Sacrifice

The symbolic meaning of life cycles in these myths is profound. Just as seeds must be buried to grow, and harvests must be reaped to sow again, the stories remind us that endings are not final. Death and sacrifice are parts of an ongoing cycle that lead to new beginnings. This understanding is reflected in the rituals, ceremonies, and artistic expressions of many cultures, where the act of giving is seen as sacred and necessary for the sustenance of life.

In Aztec culture, the importance of sacrifice was understood not as a loss, but as an essential contribution to the greater good. This perspective offers a different view of life and death—one that values the communal over the individual, emphasizing the interconnectedness of all living things and the divine forces that govern them.

Poetic Passage: The Cycle of Life

From seed to stalk, from sun to shade,
A story ancient, ever laid.
Where life gives all, and death must play,
The dance of harvest finds its way.

Xilonen calls with whisper soft,
A promise kept, a heart aloft.
Her golden hair, the corn's sweet grace,
A cycle spun in time's embrace.

In autumn's glean, the fields are bare,
Yet spring shall come, with tender care.
What falls to earth, what fades to rest,
Shall rise again, life's greatest test.

The Legacy of Sacrificial Myths in Modern Culture

While modern practices no longer include the literal sacrifices seen in ancient cultures, the themes of these myths persist. Acts of sacrifice and renewal are echoed in everyday life, from the sacrifices made by parents for their children to the communal effort required to sustain societies. The understanding that hardship and giving can lead to collective prosperity remains a powerful lesson.

These myths also continue to inspire art, literature, and religious practices. The symbolism of planting seeds, nurturing growth, and harvesting remains relevant as a metaphor for personal and collective transformation. The idea that life's most profound moments are intertwined with sacrifice and the promise of renewal speaks to the resilience of the human spirit.

Conclusion: The Eternal Sacrifice for Abundance

The myths of Xilonen, Demeter, Inanna, and other figures teach us that life is a cycle governed by the balance of giving and receiving, death and rebirth. The act of sacrifice, whether through ritual, personal suffering, or metaphorical planting, is shown as a sacred duty that ensures the continuation of life and prosperity. These legends remind us that the abundance we seek often comes at a cost, one that is borne with gratitude and reverence for the cycles that sustain us.

The themes of sacrifice and renewal remain timeless, offering insight into the human experience and our place within the natural world. By understanding these myths, we gain a deeper appreciation for the interconnectedness of all life, the labor that sustains it, and the profound beauty of cycles that repeat through time, each with its promise of rebirth.

Chapter 16: Shared Motifs Across Cultures

Harvest myths from around the world, despite emerging from vastly different geographies and cultural contexts, often share strikingly similar motifs. Central themes such as mother figures, life-giving deities, and cycles of death and rebirth recur in these myths, reflecting universal truths about human reliance on nature and the cycles of life. This chapter delves into the common motifs found in harvest myths across cultures, exploring their symbolic significance and cultural context. A comparative analysis will illuminate the shared human experience represented in these stories, while thematic poetry will capture their essence.

The Mother Figure: Nurturers of Life

One of the most prominent motifs in harvest myths is the mother figure, often depicted as the nurturing force behind agricultural fertility and abundance. These mother figures symbolize the earth's fertility and the life-giving properties of nature.

Demeter (Greek Mythology)

Demeter, the Greek goddess of agriculture, grain, and harvest, is one of the most well-known mother figures in mythology. Her story, centered around the abduction of her daughter Persephone by Hades, illustrates her role as the provider of nourishment and her deep connection to the cycles of life and death. When Persephone is taken to the underworld, Demeter's grief causes the earth to become barren, representing the seasonal dying of crops. Her joy upon Persephone's return symbolizes the rebirth of the land in spring, underscoring the mother figure as a symbol of fertility, resilience, and unconditional love.

Pachamama (Andean Mythology)

In Andean mythology, Pachamama, or Mother Earth, is revered as the goddess of fertility and the protector of crops and livestock. She embodies the nurturing aspects of nature, offering sustenance and shelter. Pachamama's connection to the earth is intimate, symbolizing the idea that life and prosperity are gifts from the earth that must be respected and protected. Offerings are made to her in rituals such as *Pago a la*

Tierra (Payment to the Earth), demonstrating the reciprocal relationship between humans and the earth.

Other Examples

Mother figures appear across various cultures in different forms, such as Renenutet, the Egyptian goddess of nourishment, and Brigid, the Celtic goddess of fire and fertility. These deities share common attributes of nurturing, protection, and the ability to sustain life through their connection to the earth.

Analysis: The mother figure in harvest myths represents the earth's inherent ability to nurture life. These myths reflect the understanding that human survival depends on the earth's fertility and that this relationship must be honored and maintained. The motif of the mother goddess reinforces themes of gratitude, reciprocity, and the sacred nature of the land.

Poetic Passage: The Earthly Mother

In every seed, a mother's care,
Her whispers bloom in sunlit air.
From Gaia's cradle to Pachamama's song,
Her hands have shaped the harvest strong.

Through winter's sleep and spring's delight,
She holds the world in tender might.
A gift of grain, a promise kept,
In her embrace, all life has slept.

Life-Giving Deities: Providers of Sustenance

Life-giving deities are another recurring motif in harvest myths. These gods and goddesses are often depicted as bestowing the knowledge and tools needed for agriculture, ensuring the survival and prosperity of their people.

Shennong (Chinese Mythology)

Shennong, the Divine Farmer in Chinese mythology, is celebrated as the god who introduced agriculture and herbal medicine to humanity. He taught people how to cultivate crops and identify medicinal plants, symbolizing the gift of sustenance and health. Shennong's teachings were essential for the development of agrarian society and reflect the belief that the gods provide not only food but the knowledge needed to sustain life.

Osiris (Egyptian Mythology)

Osiris, the god of the afterlife and vegetation, played a critical role in ancient Egyptian beliefs about life, death, and renewal. His story, which involves his murder by Set and subsequent resurrection by Isis, symbolizes the cycles of nature, where death is followed by new life. Osiris was associated with the Nile's annual flooding, which brought fertile soil essential for growing crops. He was seen as a life-giving force who ensured the abundance of the harvest.

Other Life-Givers

In Hindu mythology, the goddess Annapurna is the deity of food and nourishment. She embodies the life-giving aspect of the divine, ensuring that no one goes hungry. The name *Annapurna* means "full of food" or "provider of food," highlighting the theme of sustenance provided by a benevolent deity.

Analysis: Life-giving deities serve as intermediaries between the divine and the mortal world, embodying the idea that sustenance is a sacred gift. These myths emphasize the importance of gratitude and acknowledgment of the divine source of nourishment. The presence of life-giving deities in various cultures underscores the universal belief that life and prosperity are blessings to be respected and cherished.

Poetic Passage: The Gift of Life

Through fields of gold, a whisper spreads,
Of ancient gods and sacred threads.
Shennong's hand and Osiris's might,
Bring forth the grain, the day, the night.

From deities' breath, the seeds are cast,
Life's cycle turns, both slow and fast.
In harvests ripe, their stories blend,
A gift of life that knows no end.

Death-Rebirth Cycles: The Eternal Return

The motif of death and rebirth is central to many harvest myths, reflecting the agricultural cycle where crops are sown, grow, die, and are reborn in the next season. This cycle mirrors broader beliefs about life, death, and the continuity of existence.

The Maize God (Mayan Mythology)

The Mayan Maize God, *Hun Hunahpu*, embodies the concept of death and rebirth. His journey to the underworld, sacrifice, and eventual resurrection symbolize the process of planting maize, where seeds are buried in the ground (death) and later sprout to bring forth new life (rebirth). This story highlights the belief that life is cyclical, and death is not an end but a necessary phase for renewal.

Inanna (Sumerian Mythology)

Inanna's descent to the underworld is another powerful representation of the death-rebirth motif. She willingly sacrifices her status and power, passing through the seven gates of the underworld to reach her sister, Ereshkigal. Once there, she is killed and hung on a hook, symbolizing the ultimate surrender to death. However, through divine intervention, Inanna is resurrected and returns to the world above, bringing with her the promise of new life and fertility. This story illustrates that renewal often requires sacrifice and transformation.

Persephone (Greek Mythology)

The story of Persephone, mentioned earlier, also embodies the death-rebirth cycle. Her time in the underworld represents the dormancy of crops during winter, while her return signifies spring and the renewal of growth. This myth reinforces the idea that life's cycles are governed by periods of loss and return, each vital for the balance of nature.

Analysis: The death-rebirth motif in harvest myths speaks to the natural order and the inevitability of change. It teaches that death is not to be feared but understood as a part of the larger cycle of life. This motif resonates deeply with agricultural societies that rely on the annual cycle of planting, growth, and harvest. It reminds us of the resilience inherent in nature and the hope that follows periods of darkness and loss.

Poetic Passage: The Eternal Return

Deep in the soil, a secret sleeps,
A whispered tale that nature keeps.
The seed must fall, the stalk must break,
For life to rise, for dawn to wake.

Inanna's path, Persephone's call,
Through shadow's hold and winter's thrall.
Yet spring shall bloom, and hope shall spin,
The cycle turns, begins again.

Comparative Cultural Analysis

Despite the diversity of cultures and geographical distances, the common motifs found in harvest myths reveal shared human experiences and beliefs. The mother figure, life-giving deities, and death-rebirth cycles all speak to humanity's deep-rooted connection to the land and the understanding that life is a series of beginnings and endings, continuously renewed through cycles of nature.

Universal Themes

1. **Nurturance and Protection**: The motif of the mother goddess reflects the human need for care, protection, and sustenance. This figure's universality underscores the belief that the earth itself is a nurturing force that must be respected and preserved.

2. **Divine Providence**: Life-giving deities reinforce the notion that survival and prosperity are linked to the benevolence of divine forces. This motif reflects the gratitude and reverence humans feel toward the natural world and its gifts.

3. **Acceptance of Cycles**: The death-rebirth motif teaches acceptance of life's transience and the resilience to endure periods of loss. It embodies hope and renewal, reminding humanity that life continues despite moments of darkness.

Conclusion: The Shared Language of Harvest Myths

The shared motifs of mother figures, life-giving deities, and death-rebirth cycles in harvest myths from different cultures reveal a universal language of understanding. These stories are not just tales of gods and goddesses; they are reflections of humanity's relationship with nature, the divine, and the cycles that govern existence. They remind us of the essential truth that life is a continuous cycle of nurturing, labor, loss, and rebirth. By celebrating these motifs, cultures emphasize the importance of gratitude, resilience, and harmony with the natural world.

The similarities across cultures underscore the interconnectedness of human experience. They show that despite different traditions and beliefs, humanity shares a collective understanding of the sacred cycles that sustain life. The myths and motifs remind us that we are all bound by the same universal rhythms—an eternal dance that connects us to each other and to the earth that nourishes us.

Final Poetic Passage: The Harvest's Shared Voice

Across the world, in tales retold,
Of grain and gods and mothers bold.
A common voice, an ancient plea,
To sow, to reap, to live, to be.

From Shennong's gift to Ceres's grain,
To Pachamama's gentle reign.
Each story speaks of life's great span,
The dance of seed, the touch of man.

Through death and dark, through birth and light,
The myths remind, through day and night.
That in the soil, the heart, the sky,
The cycles turn, they never die.

Chapter 17: Celebrations and Rituals of Gratitude

Harvest seasons have long been marked by celebrations and rituals that express gratitude for the bounty of the earth. Across cultures, these celebrations are infused with ceremonies, festivals, and rites dedicated to harvest goddesses and agricultural deities who are believed to bless the land and ensure prosperity. From Native American Thanksgiving ceremonies to the European festival of Lammas, these rituals embody the spirit of gratitude and the deep bond between humanity and nature. This chapter will delve into the ways different cultures honor their harvest goddesses and give thanks for the fruits of the land, exploring the symbolic meanings behind these celebrations and their modern interpretations.

Native American Thanksgiving Ceremonies

For many Native American tribes, giving thanks is not limited to a single day but is an integral part of daily life and cultural practices. The harvest season, however, is a special time for expressing collective gratitude to the spirits and deities who watch over the crops and ensure their growth. One such deity is *Corn Mother*, a revered figure in many Native American myths who embodies the spirit of maize and sustenance.

The Green Corn Ceremony (Southeastern Tribes)

The Green Corn Ceremony, known as *Posketv* among the Muscogee (Creek) Nation and celebrated by other Southeastern tribes such as the Cherokee and Seminole, is one of the most significant harvest rituals. It marks the ripening of the first ears of corn and serves as both a celebration of abundance and a spiritual renewal. The ceremony involves dancing, feasting, and rituals of purification, including fasting and cleansing through sweat lodges.

Central to the Green Corn Ceremony is the act of forgiveness and the renewal of relationships within the community. This spiritual aspect reflects the belief that just as the land renews itself and brings forth new life, so must the community renew its bonds and cleanse itself of past grievances.

Thanksgiving Rituals and Symbolism

Many Native American tribes have their own versions of Thanksgiving ceremonies, which often center on offerings and prayers to deities such as Corn Mother or Earth Mother. These ceremonies include the use of sacred songs, dances, and communal feasts that honor the spirits of the land and the ancestors who have passed down agricultural knowledge. The offerings may include corn, tobacco, and other crops, symbolizing the reciprocity between humans and the divine forces that sustain them.

Symbolic Meaning: The rituals emphasize the importance of gratitude, not just for the harvest but for the interconnectedness of all life. They underscore the belief that humans are stewards of the land, responsible for maintaining harmony and balance. Gratitude in Native American traditions is a continuous practice, reinforcing the idea that the earth's gifts must be met with respect and acknowledgment.

Lammas: The European Festival of First Fruits

In Europe, Lammas, or *Lughnasadh*, is one of the oldest and most significant harvest festivals. Celebrated on August 1st, Lammas marks the beginning of the grain harvest and is associated with the Celtic god Lugh and various harvest goddesses, including Demeter and Ceres. The festival's name derives from the Old English *hlaf-mas*, meaning "loaf mass," signifying the offering of the first loaf of bread made from the newly harvested grain.

Rituals and Traditions of Lammas

Lammas is a celebration of abundance and the culmination of hard work in the fields. The festival includes the baking of bread, which is often blessed and shared among the community as a symbol of unity and sustenance. In some traditions, the first sheaf of wheat is woven into a corn dolly, representing the spirit of the harvest. This figure is kept until the next planting season, when it is plowed into the field as an offering to ensure future fertility.

Bonfires and feasting are common during Lammas, serving as a way for communities to come together and give thanks. Music, dancing, and storytelling are integral parts of the celebration, linking the present to the past and reinforcing cultural traditions.

The Role of Harvest Goddesses

Goddesses like Demeter and Ceres are often invoked during Lammas. Demeter, in Greek mythology, presides over the harvest and embodies the nurturing and protective qualities of the earth. Her story, intertwined with that of her daughter Persephone, symbolizes the seasonal cycle of growth, death, and rebirth. Similarly, Ceres, the Roman goddess of agriculture, grain crops, and fertility, is honored for her role in ensuring a bountiful harvest.

Symbolic Meaning: The rituals of Lammas underscore themes of gratitude, abundance, and the cyclical nature of life. The festival represents the balance between hard work and the rewards of labor, reinforcing the idea that life's blessings come through both effort and divine favor.

The Japanese Festival of Shinto Harvest: Niinamesai

In Japan, the ancient Shinto ritual of *Niinamesai* (◇◇◇) is a harvest festival that celebrates the rice harvest and offers gratitude to the kami (spirits) for their blessings. The emperor plays a significant role in this ritual, as he performs the ceremony on behalf of the entire nation, symbolizing the unity between the divine and the people.

Rituals of Niinamesai

During the festival, the emperor presents the newly harvested rice to the kami as an offering and partakes in eating the rice himself, signifying the shared blessings between the gods and the people. The ritual is conducted in a sacred space, and the atmosphere is marked by reverence and solemnity.

The concept of *amae* (a feeling of dependence on the benevolence of others) is present in Niinamesai, reflecting the belief that humans are indebted to the kami for their continued prosperity. The festival reaffirms the bond between the natural and spiritual worlds, highlighting the importance of maintaining harmony with the environment.

Symbolic Meaning: Niinamesai reinforces themes of community, gratitude, and respect for nature. It acknowledges the divine forces that sustain life and emphasizes the importance of humility and appreciation for the gifts of the earth.

Harvest Festivals in Hindu Tradition: Pongal

Pongal is a multi-day Hindu harvest festival celebrated primarily in the southern Indian state of Tamil Nadu. Dedicated to the sun god Surya, Pongal signifies the end of the winter solstice and the beginning of the sun's northward journey, marking the season of harvest. The festival's name comes from the Tamil word *pongal*, which means "to boil over," referring to the traditional dish made from rice, milk, and jaggery.

Rituals and Celebrations

Pongal is marked by a series of rituals that express gratitude to the deities, especially Surya, for a successful harvest. On the first day, called *Bhogi*, people discard old possessions and celebrate the new, symbolizing renewal and transformation. The main day, *Thai Pongal*, involves boiling rice and milk in a pot until it overflows, symbolizing prosperity and abundance. Families gather to watch the boiling pot and shout "Pongalo Pongal!" as a collective expression of joy and gratitude.

The third day, *Mattu Pongal*, is dedicated to honoring cattle, which play a vital role in agriculture. Cows and oxen are decorated with garlands and their horns painted, showing respect for their contribution to the harvest.

Symbolic Meaning: Pongal celebrates the relationship between humans, nature, and the divine. The overflowing pot symbolizes prosperity, while the rituals acknowledge the interconnectedness of all life forms in the agricultural cycle.

Modern Interpretations and Revivals of Harvest Celebrations

In the contemporary world, many traditional harvest celebrations have evolved or been revived to adapt to modern times. Community harvest festivals and cultural events often include elements of ancient rituals, such as communal meals, dances, and offerings. These events serve as reminders of the importance of gratitude, community, and a connection to the land, even in urbanized societies.

Thanksgiving in the United States

Thanksgiving, as celebrated in the United States, has its roots in harvest celebrations. Although it has become a secular holiday focused on family gatherings and feasting, it echoes the themes of gratitude found in earlier harvest rituals. Native American harvest celebrations, with their deep respect for the land and its bounty, influenced the original Thanksgiving feasts shared with European settlers. Today, Thanksgiving continues to serve as a time to reflect on blessings, express gratitude, and share abundance with others.

The Cultural Significance of Harvest Rituals

Harvest rituals and celebrations share common themes of gratitude, community, and the cyclical nature of life. These practices reinforce the idea that human existence is intimately connected with the rhythms of the earth and that the gifts of the land must be honored. Whether through elaborate festivals, communal prayers, or simple acts of sharing, the spirit of these rituals persists across cultures and time.

Shared Lessons and Modern Relevance:

1. **Gratitude as a Universal Practice**: Harvest rituals remind us to practice gratitude not just during festivals but throughout our daily lives.
2. **Community Bonds**: These celebrations emphasize the importance of coming together, reinforcing that the prosperity of one depends on the collective strength of all.

3. **Harmony with Nature**: Harvest rituals teach that nature's cycles are sacred and that human survival depends on respecting and nurturing the environment.

Conclusion: Celebrating the Cycle of Life

Harvest celebrations and rituals of gratitude highlight the enduring connection between humans, nature, and the divine. From the Native American Thanksgiving ceremonies that honor Corn Mother to the European festival of Lammas, the Japanese *Niinamesai*, and the Hindu festival of Pongal, these traditions emphasize themes of abundance, community, and respect for the natural world. Modern interpretations of these rituals continue to draw on ancient practices, reminding us of the deep-rooted values that sustain human societies.

As we move further into an age where technology and urbanization dominate, the lessons from these harvest celebrations remain vital. They encourage us to pause, give thanks, and remember that the earth's gifts are not guaranteed but must be nurtured and cherished. By honoring these traditions, we maintain a link to our ancestors and the timeless truths they held—that life is a cycle of giving and receiving, and that gratitude is the seed from which prosperity and harmony grow.

Final Poetic Passage: The Harvest Song

In fields of gold, where stories lie,
We gather 'neath the autumn sky.
With songs of thanks and hearts alight,
We celebrate the harvest's might.

From Corn Mother's grace to Ceres's grain,
To Surya's sun and Pachamama's rain.
The earth gives all, a gift so pure,
A bond we hold, both strong and sure.

May rituals old and new inspire,
To live with love and hearts afire.
For in each seed, in each bright flame,
We find the world, we find her name.

Chapter 18: Harvest Myths in Modern Storytelling

Ancient harvest myths, deeply rooted in the cycles of life, death, and renewal, have transcended time and culture to inspire modern literature, art, and storytelling. These myths, with their powerful symbols and themes, continue to resonate because they speak to fundamental aspects of human existence: sustenance, gratitude, and the eternal return of life after loss. This chapter explores how ancient harvest myths have influenced contemporary media and discusses examples that demonstrate their lasting impact on modern storytelling.

The Timeless Appeal of Harvest Myths

Harvest myths are rich in symbolism, making them ideal sources of inspiration for modern storytelling. Central to these myths are universal themes such as sacrifice, rebirth, and the nurturing aspect of nature. These themes are relevant today as they address both personal and collective human experiences, such as the struggle for survival, the importance of community, and the hope that follows hardship.

The motifs of life-giving deities, mother figures, and the death-rebirth cycle have found new life in contemporary media. Writers, filmmakers, and artists draw on these ancient stories to create narratives that are familiar yet infused with modern sensibilities. The result is a body of work that bridges the gap between ancient tradition and modern interpretation, keeping the essence of these myths alive.

Modern Literature Inspired by Harvest Myths

Contemporary literature is rich with works that echo the motifs and themes of ancient harvest myths. These stories often reimagine or reinterpret the original myths, adding new layers of meaning that resonate with today's audiences.

Margaret Atwood's *The Year of the Flood*

Margaret Atwood's *The Year of the Flood* is part of her *MaddAddam* trilogy, a series that explores themes of environmental collapse, renewal, and human resilience. The story draws on ancient motifs of death and rebirth, echoing the cycles of nature seen in harvest myths. Atwood's narrative incorporates religious rituals performed by the "God's Gardeners," a group that reveres nature and practices sustainable living. Their ceremonies and hymns are reminiscent of the rituals dedicated to deities like Demeter, Ceres, and Pachamama, reflecting a respect for the cycles of the earth and the interconnectedness of all life.

The depiction of nature as both a nurturing and destructive force mirrors the dual nature of agricultural deities and reinforces the idea that humans are both dependent on and at the mercy of the natural world. The novel's themes of sacrifice and renewal draw clear parallels to myths where life must be given to ensure the continuity of life, such as the Aztec tales of Xilonen and the Greek story of Persephone.

Neil Gaiman's *American Gods*

Neil Gaiman's *American Gods* is a modern narrative that draws on myths from various cultures, integrating them into a contemporary setting. The character of Easter (Ostara), a goddess associated with spring and renewal, embodies the life-giving aspects of mother figures in harvest myths. Gaiman's portrayal of deities who are weakened due to the lack of belief reflects the idea that abundance and prosperity are tied to human reverence and ritual. This echoes ancient practices where the success of the harvest was believed to depend on proper offerings and ceremonies to the gods.

The novel's exploration of forgotten gods and the resurgence of old beliefs highlights the timeless nature of these myths and their relevance in modern society. The themes of death and rebirth are prominent, emphasizing the cyclical nature of life that is central to harvest mythology.

Harvest Motifs in Modern Art

Modern art continues to draw inspiration from the themes of harvest myths, often using visual elements to explore the relationships between humanity, nature, and the divine. The symbolism of the seed, the cycle of planting and harvesting, and the figure of the nurturing mother appear in various forms of visual art.

The Works of Frida Kahlo

Frida Kahlo's art, while deeply personal, frequently incorporates themes that resonate with harvest myths. Her use of natural imagery, such as flowers, fruits, and roots, reflects the cycles of growth, death, and rebirth. In works like *Roots*, Kahlo paints herself as being intertwined with the earth, symbolizing nourishment and regeneration. This imagery evokes the nurturing aspect of mother deities such as Demeter and Pachamama, as well as the idea that life and sustenance are inseparable from the earth.

Kahlo's exploration of suffering and renewal parallels the themes found in myths where sacrifice leads to abundance. Her art often portrays the duality of life and death, reminiscent of the death-rebirth cycles seen in myths about Inanna's descent to the underworld or the resurrection of Osiris.

Film and Television: Harvest Myths Reimagined

Film and television provide a dynamic medium for retelling and reimagining harvest myths. These stories often use visual and narrative techniques to bring ancient themes to life, appealing to modern audiences while maintaining the essence of the original myths.

***The Hunger Games* Series**

Suzanne Collins' *The Hunger Games* series, while not a direct retelling of an ancient harvest myth, embodies many of the themes found in these stories. The plot revolves around a society where sacrifice is required to maintain control and ensure the survival of the ruling class. Katniss Everdeen's role as the "Mockingjay" symbolizes both the hope for renewal and the willingness to sacrifice for the greater good, echoing the sacrificial themes found in myths like that of Xilonen and Persephone.

The series also explores the importance of food, sustenance, and survival, drawing on the idea that life is sustained through the cyclical nature of growth and harvest. The bleak, dystopian setting emphasizes the consequences of humanity's disconnection from nature and the life-sustaining practices that were central to ancient harvest rituals.

The Wicker Man **(1973)**

The original film *The Wicker Man* (1973) is a psychological horror film that draws heavily on themes of sacrifice and renewal. The story centers around a Scottish village that practices ancient pagan rituals to ensure a successful harvest. The motif of sacrificing a life to appease the gods and secure the community's prosperity is central to the narrative and directly parallels ancient myths of offerings made to deities like Demeter or the Aztec gods.

The film's climax, where the protagonist is sacrificed to bring fertility back to the land, starkly reflects the belief that abundance often requires a significant sacrifice. This echoes the ancient practice of human and animal sacrifice found in many cultures, where life was given to sustain life.

Thematic Analysis: Why Harvest Myths Endure

Harvest myths endure in modern storytelling because they encapsulate essential truths about the human experience. They speak to our relationship with the earth, our dependence on its cycles, and the rituals we create to ensure survival. The themes of sacrifice, renewal, and gratitude continue to resonate because they are universal. They reflect the challenges and rewards of existence and remind us that life's cycles are both inevitable and sacred.

These myths also serve as cautionary tales and moral lessons. They remind us that prosperity comes with responsibilities—that balance must be maintained, and respect for the natural world is paramount. In a modern context, where environmental sustainability is a pressing issue, the motifs in harvest myths encourage reflection on humanity's impact on the earth and the importance of stewardship.

Conclusion: The Lasting Legacy of Harvest Myths

Harvest myths have woven themselves into the fabric of modern storytelling, manifesting in literature, art, film, and television. Their motifs of mother figures, life-giving deities, and cycles of death and rebirth continue to capture the imagination because they address fundamental aspects of the human condition. These stories remind us of the timeless nature of human challenges—our reliance on the earth for sustenance, the sacrifices made for survival, and the hope for renewal after hardship.

As we face modern challenges such as environmental degradation and climate change, the lessons from these myths remain relevant. They inspire us to view the earth as a living entity that must be respected and cared for, just as ancient cultures believed. Through modern storytelling, the legacy of harvest myths endures, bridging the past and the present and reminding us that the cycles of life, sacrifice, and renewal are universal and eternal.

Final Poetic Passage: The Myth's Legacy

Old stories bloom in new designs,
In art that echoes ancient signs.
From Demeter's tears to Katniss' fight,
The seed is sown, in dark and light.

Sacrifice, a tale retold,
In harvest myths, both new and old.
The earth, a mother, fierce and wise,
Holds lessons deep, in field and skies.

In every story, root and vine,
The ancient truths, a thread divine.
Through cycles spun, and tales retold,
We learn again what ancients told.

Chapter 19: Poetic Reflections on Harvest Themes

The stories and myths of harvests shared throughout this book are steeped in themes of nurturing, sacrifice, and renewal. These themes speak to the universal experiences of growth, sustenance, loss, and hope that resonate across cultures and time. This chapter presents a compilation of original poetry that captures the essence of these harvest themes, weaving together the stories of mother figures, life-giving deities, and the cycles of death and rebirth.

The Earth's Embrace

Beneath the soil, a silent prayer,
The earth's embrace, both warm and rare.
In tender care, a seed is laid,
A promise kept, a hope conveyed.

With whispers soft and shadows deep,
The roots will stretch, the vines will creep.
For what is sown with heart and hand,
Returns with life across the land.

O gentle mother, source and seed,
Your touch provides, fulfills each need.
From grain to fruit, from bloom to bread,
You are the feast where all are fed.

Song of the Maize God

Hun Hunahpu, in fields of gold,
Your story ancient, never old.
Through underworld, through dark and flame,
You rose again, we speak your name.

Sacrifice, your gift so vast,
From death's embrace, life's roots are cast.
The green shoots rise, the people sing,
For in your tale, rebirth does spring.

Maize of life, and god of grace,
In every kernel, time's embrace.
We honor you in toil and feast,
The sowing done, the harvest ceased.

The Cycle of Persephone

Beneath the earth, Persephone sleeps,
In shadowed halls where silence creeps.
A mother mourns, the fields lie bare,
Winter's breath in frosted air.

But spring shall come with golden light,
And bring her forth from Hades' night.
Demeter's tears, once cold and still,
Will water life upon the hill.

The wheel turns round, from death to birth,
A sacred bond between the earth.
Each season's grief, each season's joy,
A mother's hope, a daughter's ploy.

The Feast of Lammas

First loaf broken, shared with care,
The taste of toil, the warmth of prayer.
In August's glow, the fields once green,
Give forth their gold, a sight serene.

A corn dolly stands, woven tight,
A spirit kept through autumn's bite.
She watches o'er the reaping done,
As songs are sung, and tales begun.

Demeter smiles as bread is blessed,
A harvest queen, in ritual dressed.
For every grain and every ear,
Holds whispers of the turning year.

The Dance of Inanna

Through gates of stone, Inanna passed,
Her robes removed, her power cast.
In shadow's grip, she faced the night,
In silence deep, without her light.

But from her fall, the seeds did rise,
New shoots of green, beneath the skies.
From death's embrace, from sorrow's hue,
Life's tender breath was born anew.

The harvest came, the people sang,
With gifts of grain where echoes rang.
For in her dance, they saw the truth,
That death's dark path leads back to youth.

Pachamama's Song

Mother of mountains, river, and stone,
Your voice in wind, your heart our home.
From Andean peaks, your blessings flow,
Where fields of quinoa thrive and grow.
We offer leaves and coca sweet,
At sacred shrines where earth and sky meet.
You cradle life in arms so wide,
Each grain and seed, in you abide.
Pachamama, in sun's embrace,
Your spirit moves in every space.
The harvest dance, the people's cheer,
Honor the life you hold so dear.

The Offering of Xilonen

Drums that echo, songs that soar,
Xilonen's name we all implore.
Maiden crowned with golden hair,
Guardian of maize, both rich and rare.
The sacrifice, the blood, the fire,
A ritual born of deep desire.
To bring the rain, to bless the land,
To reap the crops with gentle hand.
O goddess young, in fields you play,
Your spirit guides both night and day.

In every ear, your story weaves,
A gift of life, among the sheaves.

Thanksgiving's Light

Corn Mother's grace, a tale retold,
In autumn's hues of red and gold.
The feast prepared, the circle tight,
A gathering in the fading light.

Songs of thanks, and words of praise,
For summer's sun and harvest days.
From field to plate, from heart to heart,
The cycle turns, each plays their part.

To give, to share, to bless the ground,
In every meal, a truth profound.
For what we take, we must restore,
The earth, our mother, asks no more.

The Eternal Dance of Sacrifice

In sacrifice, the seeds are sown,
A lesson deep, an echo known.
Osiris' fall, Inanna's descent,
The cost of growth, the life we've spent.

Yet from the dark, the roots will climb,
To seek the sun, in endless time.
The cycle moves, the dance begins,
Through harvest's loss, renewal wins.

Each grain that falls, each stalk that breaks,
A gift of life the earth remakes.
With every season, sorrow's cease,
Comes nature's gift—abundant peace.

Conclusion: Harvest in Verse

These poetic reflections are inspired by the myths and stories of harvest that have transcended cultures and time. The themes of nurturing, sacrifice, and renewal remind us of the delicate balance between giving and receiving, death and life, loss and abundance. Harvest myths and their modern interpretations hold powerful lessons, encouraging us to reflect on our relationship with the earth, the sacrifices that sustain us, and the perpetual hope of renewal.

These verses serve as a tribute to the universal cycle of life and the stories that continue to inspire us. The harvest, in all its forms, remains a testament to resilience, gratitude, and the sacred act of nurturing life.

Chapter 20: The Timelessness of Harvest Myths

As we reach the conclusion of this exploration of harvest myths, it becomes clear that their significance extends far beyond the ancient societies that first told them. These stories, filled with themes of nurturing, sacrifice, and renewal, remain deeply relevant in today's world. They reflect timeless truths about human existence, our relationship with the natural world, and the universal cycles that govern life. This final chapter will tie together the overarching themes of the book and explore why these myths continue to resonate in contemporary culture.

The Universal Themes of Harvest Myths

Throughout this book, we have encountered recurring motifs that transcend geographical and cultural boundaries. Whether it is the nurturing figure of Demeter mourning her daughter's descent into the underworld, the selfless sacrifice of Osiris for the fertility of the Nile, or the enduring spirit of Pachamama in Andean celebrations, harvest myths capture the essence of human experience. The core themes that emerge from these stories—nurturing, sacrifice, and renewal—speak to the universal cycles of life, death, and rebirth.

Nurturing: The Gift of the Earth

At the heart of many harvest myths is the image of the mother figure, embodying the earth's nurturing qualities. Goddesses such as Demeter, Pachamama, and Corn Mother serve as symbols of the life-giving properties of the earth. These figures remind us that humanity's survival depends on the careful stewardship of the land. In today's world, where environmental sustainability has become a global concern, these myths hold a powerful message. They teach that the earth's gifts are not to be taken for granted but cherished and protected. The nurturing aspects of these deities encourage us to consider our role as caretakers of the planet, emphasizing reciprocity and gratitude for nature's abundance.

Relevance Today: The theme of nurturing resonates with current movements advocating for sustainable agriculture, eco-friendly practices, and community-based living. The nurturing spirit found in harvest myths is reflected in modern initiatives that prioritize environmental care and the preservation of natural resources for future generations.

Sacrifice: The Cost of Abundance

Sacrifice is another prominent theme in harvest myths, illustrating that abundance often comes at a cost. The story of Xilonen, the Aztec goddess of young maize, whose rituals included offerings to secure a prosperous harvest, underscores the belief that life is sustained through acts of giving. The myths of Osiris and Inanna highlight the personal sacrifices made by these deities for the sake of renewal and the continued prosperity of their people.

In these stories, sacrifice is not portrayed as a tragic loss but as a necessary part of the cycle of life. The idea that something must be given up for growth to occur reflects the human experience of working, striving, and giving for the benefit of oneself and others. This theme is particularly relevant in a world that often emphasizes immediate gain without acknowledging the sacrifices that underpin true prosperity.

Relevance Today: The theme of sacrifice aligns with modern narratives about resilience, hard work, and the importance of community and collective welfare. In a world facing climate challenges, economic disparities, and social upheavals, the idea that lasting abundance requires sacrifice and shared effort is as relevant as ever. It encourages reflection on how individual and collective actions can contribute to greater societal good.

Renewal: The Cycle of Life and Hope

The motif of renewal is woven into the fabric of every harvest myth, from Persephone's return to the surface world to the resurrection of the Mayan Maize God, Hun Hunahpu. These stories emphasize that death is not an end but part of an eternal cycle that leads to rebirth and new life. The hope of renewal is what sustains communities through difficult times, offering the promise that after loss, there is the potential for regeneration.

The idea of renewal is powerful in contemporary society, where people often seek meaning and hope amid change and adversity. Harvest myths remind us that challenges are not insurmountable; they are simply part of life's natural ebb and flow. The concept of renewal invites us to see setbacks as opportunities for growth and transformation, fostering resilience in the face of hardship.

Relevance Today: The theme of renewal aligns with personal and collective narratives of recovery, whether it is rebuilding after natural disasters, overcoming economic downturns, or finding new ways to thrive in an ever-changing world. In a time marked by rapid change and uncertainty, the assurance that life continues and can flourish again is a source of comfort and inspiration.

The Cultural Significance of Harvest Myths in the Modern World

Harvest myths have persisted through centuries because they embody fundamental truths about human life. Their narratives serve as metaphors for the human condition, touching on themes of dependence, gratitude, and the delicate balance between giving and receiving. As we move into an age defined by technological advancement and global connectivity, these ancient stories still have much to teach us about values, community, and sustainability.

Community and Collective Gratitude

One of the most significant aspects of harvest myths is their emphasis on communal celebration and shared gratitude. Rituals like Lammas, Pongal, and Native American Thanksgiving ceremonies highlight the importance of coming together to acknowledge the bounty of the earth and express thanks. In a world where individualism often takes precedence, these myths remind us of the strength found in community and the shared responsibility of caring for the earth.

Modern Implications: Community gardens, local food movements, and shared harvest festivals are modern interpretations of ancient practices that foster a sense of unity and shared purpose. These initiatives echo the communal spirit of harvest celebrations, reinforcing the idea that the well-being of one is intertwined with the well-being of all.

The Interconnectedness of Life

Harvest myths underscore the interconnectedness of all living things, emphasizing the relationship between humans, nature, and the divine. This perspective is essential as we confront environmental issues that threaten ecosystems and biodiversity. The stories of Demeter, Pachamama, and Shennong remind us that humanity's fate is tied to the earth's health and that nurturing the planet is integral to our survival.

Modern Implications: Environmental movements and ecological education initiatives draw on the same principles found in harvest myths—recognizing that sustainability is only possible when there is respect for the cycles of nature. By teaching future generations about these ancient stories, we can instill a deeper understanding of the importance of living in harmony with the natural world.

Harvest Myths as a Source of Inspiration

In addition to their cultural and thematic significance, harvest myths continue to inspire contemporary storytelling, literature, art, and film. Modern interpretations of these myths often explore similar themes of nurturing, sacrifice, and renewal, offering new insights and perspectives. Works such as Neil Gaiman's *American Gods*, Margaret Atwood's *The Year of the Flood*, and various adaptations of Persephone's tale show that these ancient narratives still captivate and resonate with audiences today.

Creativity and Reflection: Artists, writers, and creators often draw from the motifs found in harvest myths to explore questions of human resilience, environmental ethics, and the quest for balance in life. The enduring relevance of these stories proves that they are more than relics of the past; they are dynamic sources of wisdom that continue to inspire and challenge us.

Conclusion: The Eternal Cycle of Myths and Humanity

The harvest myths explored throughout this book remind us that the cycles of planting, growth, death, and renewal are not just agricultural phenomena; they are metaphors for the human journey. The themes of nurturing, sacrifice, and renewal are woven into our daily lives, influencing how we interact with each other, how we perceive challenges, and how we relate to the world around us.

These stories have survived for millennia because they speak to our deepest instincts and values. They teach us to honor the past, respect the present, and cultivate hope for the future. In a time when humanity faces significant challenges, from climate change to social inequality, the lessons of harvest myths urge us to remember that true prosperity is built on gratitude, resilience, and the understanding that life is a cycle in which each part, no matter how difficult, plays a role in fostering growth and renewal.

The timelessness of harvest myths lies in their ability to remind us of our place in the world—connected to the earth, to each other, and to the cycles that sustain life. As we look to the future, may we carry the wisdom of these stories with us, nurturing the seeds of hope, making sacrifices for the greater good, and finding renewal in every season of life.

Final Poetic Reflection: The Cycle Unbroken

The myths we tell, the stories spun,
Of seeds and sun, of loss and won.
From ancient hearths to modern flame,
Their echoes rise, their lessons claim.

Nurture well, with tender hand,
The earth, the sea, the sky, the land.
For in the sowing, in the reap,
A promise waits, a vow to keep.

Sacrifice, the path we tread,
With gratitude for daily bread.
Renewal's hope in winter's chill,
A bloom, a breath, a life fulfilled.

So let us guard these tales so old,
Their wisdom rich, their courage bold.
In every grain and every root,
The timeless song of life's pursuit.

Appendices

Appendix A: Glossary of Deities and Terms

This appendix serves as a comprehensive guide to the deities, mythological terms, and key concepts referenced throughout the book. It provides readers with a deeper understanding of the figures and themes that shape the rich tapestry of harvest myths and their enduring legacy.

A

Amae

A Japanese concept that denotes a sense of dependence on the benevolence of others, often seen in the context of gratitude and reverence for divine or natural forces.

Annapurna

A Hindu goddess of food and nourishment. Her name means "full of food," and she is revered as the provider of sustenance, symbolizing the life-giving aspect of the divine.

Apollo

In Greek mythology, Apollo is the god of many domains, including the sun, light, music, and prophecy. He is associated with the cycles of nature and agriculture due to his connection to sunlight and its role in growth.

B

Brigid (Brighid)

A Celtic goddess of fire, fertility, healing, and poetry. Brigid is revered as a life-giving force and is connected to agricultural fertility and the nurturing aspects of the earth.

C

Ceres

The Roman goddess of agriculture, grain crops, fertility, and motherly relationships. She is equivalent to the Greek goddess Demeter and played a vital role in Roman rituals that celebrated harvest and abundance.

Corn Mother

A figure in Native American mythology associated with maize and the sustenance it provides. Corn Mother symbolizes fertility, renewal, and the nurturing qualities of the earth.

Corn Dolly

A traditional figure woven from the last sheaf of wheat harvested, used in various European harvest festivals to symbolize the spirit of the harvest. It is kept until the next planting season as a token of fertility and good luck.

D

Demeter

The Greek goddess of agriculture, grain, and the harvest. She is the mother of Persephone, and her grief over Persephone's abduction by Hades is the origin of the changing seasons in Greek mythology.

Divine Farmer (Shennong)

A legendary figure in Chinese mythology, credited with teaching people the practice of agriculture and the use of medicinal herbs. Shennong is considered a life-giving deity who ensured the survival and prosperity of humanity through the introduction of crops.

E

Ereshkigal

The Sumerian goddess of the underworld and the sister of Inanna. Ereshkigal's realm symbolizes death and the end of life's cycle, contrasting with Inanna's association with life and fertility.

G

Gaia

The personification of the earth in Greek mythology. Gaia is considered the mother of all life and is central to myths involving creation and fertility.

Green Corn Ceremony

A significant harvest festival among Southeastern Native American tribes, such as the Muscogee and Cherokee. It is a time of renewal, forgiveness, and gratitude for the harvest, particularly maize.

H

Hun Hunahpu (Mayan Maize God)

A key deity in Mayan mythology associated with maize, fertility, and life. His journey through the underworld and subsequent resurrection symbolizes the cyclical nature of agriculture and the renewal of life.

I

Imbolc

A Celtic festival held at the beginning of February to celebrate the midpoint between the winter solstice and spring equinox. It is associated with the goddess Brigid and marks the preparation for spring and the renewal of the earth.

Inanna

A Sumerian goddess of love, fertility, and war. Her descent into the underworld and subsequent resurrection is a powerful myth representing death and rebirth, echoing the themes found in harvest rituals and the cycles of nature.

L

Lammas (Lughnasadh)

An ancient European festival held on August 1st to celebrate the beginning of the grain harvest. It is associated with baking bread from the first harvested grain and making offerings to deities such as Lugh, Demeter, and Ceres.

Lugh

A Celtic god associated with the harvest festival Lughnasadh. Lugh is known for his skills in many areas, including craftsmanship and agriculture, and is considered a protector of crops and prosperity.

M

Mattu Pongal

The third day of the South Indian harvest festival Pongal, dedicated to honoring cattle, which play an essential role in agriculture. Cows and oxen are adorned with garlands and their horns are painted in recognition of their contribution to the harvest.

Mother Earth (Pachamama)

A revered Andean deity representing the earth and fertility. Pachamama is central to the spiritual practices of indigenous Andean communities and is celebrated in rituals like *Pago a la Tierra* (Payment to the Earth), which express gratitude for her sustenance.

N

Niinamesai

An ancient Shinto harvest ritual in Japan where the emperor offers newly harvested rice to the kami (spirits) as an expression of gratitude and respect. The ceremony symbolizes the unity between the divine, the emperor, and the people.

O

Orisha Oko

In Yoruba mythology, Orisha Oko is the god of agriculture and the harvest. He is invoked for the fertility of the land and the success of crops.

Osiris

The Egyptian god of the afterlife and vegetation. Osiris is associated with the Nile's annual flooding and the growth of crops, symbolizing death and resurrection.

P

Pachamama

See **Mother Earth (Pachamama)**.

Persephone

The Greek goddess of spring and the queen of the underworld. Persephone's abduction by Hades and subsequent return to her mother Demeter explain the cycle of the seasons. Her story embodies themes of loss, rebirth, and renewal.

Pongal

A Hindu harvest festival celebrated primarily in Tamil Nadu, India. It is dedicated to Surya, the sun god, and includes rituals of boiling rice and milk to signify prosperity.

Posketv

See **Green Corn Ceremony**.

R

Renenutet

An Egyptian goddess associated with nourishment and the protection of crops. She was believed to ensure the fertility of the fields and the abundance of the harvest.

S

Sacrifice

A recurring theme in many harvest myths, where deities or people offer something valuable to secure a bountiful harvest or to appease the gods. This concept underscores the belief that prosperity often requires giving up something in return.

Surya

The Hindu sun god who plays a crucial role in agricultural rituals, such as Pongal. Surya's energy is believed to nourish the earth and enable the growth of crops.

T

Tonalli

In Aztec belief, *tonalli* refers to a vital life force or energy that exists in all living things. Sacrificial offerings were thought to release this energy, ensuring the favor of the gods and the fertility of the land.

X

Xilonen

The Aztec goddess of young maize and a symbol of fertility and growth. Rituals in her honor often included sacrifices to secure a successful harvest.

Z

Zemlya Mat' (Mother Earth)

The Slavic goddess representing the earth and its fertility. Similar to Pachamama and Demeter, Zemlya Mat' embodies the nurturing and life-giving properties of nature.

Glossary Conclusion

This glossary provides insight into the many deities, mythological terms, and concepts mentioned throughout the book. These figures and themes highlight the universality of harvest myths, emphasizing the shared human experience of honoring the cycles of nature, giving thanks for sustenance, and recognizing the sacrifices that ensure prosperity. Through understanding these terms, readers can better appreciate the enduring legacy of harvest myths and their significance in both ancient and modern contexts.

Appendix B: Cultural and Historical Contexts

Understanding the cultural and historical contexts of harvest myths enriches our appreciation of their significance and the values they embody. This appendix provides background information on the civilizations and traditions that shaped the myths explored in the book. By examining the societies that birthed these stories, readers can gain insight into how agricultural practices, environmental conditions, and religious beliefs influenced the creation and perpetuation of these enduring myths.

1. Ancient Greece

Cultural and Agricultural Significance: Ancient Greece was a civilization deeply intertwined with nature and the rhythms of the agricultural calendar. Agriculture was the backbone of the Greek economy, with crops like wheat, barley, olives, and grapes playing central roles. The Greeks relied heavily on seasonal changes, and the success of their harvests was critical to their survival.

Religious Beliefs: The Greeks practiced polytheism and believed that their gods and goddesses played active roles in influencing the natural world. Demeter, the goddess of agriculture and harvest, was central to their religious practices, symbolizing the earth's fertility and the nurturing aspects of the mother. The myth of Demeter and Persephone explained the seasonal cycle and reflected the Greeks' deep respect for the land and the life it provided.

Festivals and Rituals: The *Thesmophoria* was a prominent festival dedicated to Demeter and Persephone, focusing on themes of fertility and renewal. This multi-day event involved rituals, offerings, and prayers to ensure the earth's productivity and honor the goddesses' roles in sustaining life.

2. The Roman Empire

Cultural and Agricultural Practices: The Roman Empire expanded upon Greek agricultural traditions, adapting them to their own deities and social customs. Agriculture was a vital part of Roman life, with the cultivation of grain being essential to feeding its growing population. Roman farmers practiced crop rotation and advanced irrigation methods to maximize yields.

Deities and Beliefs: Ceres, the Roman goddess of agriculture and fertility, was akin to the Greek Demeter. The worship of Ceres emphasized the importance of grain, and rituals were conducted to ensure a successful harvest. The *Cerealia*, an annual festival in her honor, included processions, games, and sacrifices, reflecting the critical role agriculture played in Roman society.

Historical Context: The Roman Empire's emphasis on agricultural prosperity was not only for sustenance but also for maintaining political stability. Grain shortages often led to social unrest, making the favor of agricultural deities like Ceres crucial to maintaining peace and order.

3. Ancient Egypt

Environmental Conditions: Ancient Egypt's agriculture was deeply dependent on the annual flooding of the Nile River. This natural event deposited nutrient-rich silt on the land, enabling the Egyptians to grow crops such as wheat, barley, and flax. The predictability of the Nile's flooding was central to the development of their agricultural society.

Religious Practices: The Egyptians believed that the gods were responsible for the natural world's balance. Osiris, the god of the afterlife and vegetation, was a key figure in their mythology. His death and resurrection symbolized the cycle of the Nile's flooding, the planting of seeds, and the eventual harvest. The story of Osiris and his wife, Isis, underscored themes of sacrifice, renewal, and the continuity of life.

Festivals and Offerings: Rituals and festivals associated with Osiris often involved processions, symbolic re-enactments of his myth, and offerings of grain. These practices reinforced the connection between the people and the divine, highlighting the belief that agricultural abundance was a sacred gift.

4. Mesoamerican Civilizations: The Maya and the Aztecs

Mayan Context: The Maya civilization flourished in the region that is now southeastern Mexico, Guatemala, Belize, and parts of Honduras and El Salvador. Their culture was rich in agricultural practices, with maize being the central crop. The Mayan creation story in the *Popol Vuh* describes humans as being created from maize dough, emphasizing its sacred status.

Religious Beliefs: The Mayan Maize God, *Hun Hunahpu*, was an essential figure representing life, fertility, and sustenance. His myth, which involves death, journeying through the underworld, and resurrection, symbolized the planting, growth, and harvesting of maize. Rituals and ceremonies often included offerings and dances to honor the Maize God and ensure bountiful crops.

Aztec Context: The Aztecs inhabited central Mexico and developed complex agricultural systems, including chinampas (floating gardens) to maximize arable land. Their society was highly structured, with religious practices deeply embedded in daily life.

Deities and Sacrifice: Xilonen, the goddess of young maize, and Tlaloc, the rain god, were central to Aztec agricultural practices. The Aztecs believed that the gods sacrificed themselves to create the world, which influenced their ritual practices involving human and animal sacrifices. These offerings were believed to maintain cosmic balance and ensure the gods' favor for a successful harvest.

5. The Andean Civilizations

Geography and Agriculture: The Andean region, home to civilizations like the Inca, had a challenging landscape of mountains and high-altitude plains. The Incas developed advanced agricultural techniques, such as terracing and irrigation, to cultivate crops like maize, potatoes, and quinoa.

Religious Practices: Pachamama, or Mother Earth, was a central figure in Andean spiritual beliefs. She was considered the provider of life and sustenance, embodying the earth's fertility and nurturing qualities. The *Pago a la Tierra* ritual involved offerings of coca leaves, chicha (a traditional drink), and other items to Pachamama, expressing gratitude and ensuring her favor for future harvests.

Cultural Significance: The Andean peoples viewed agriculture as a sacred practice that connected them to the natural and spiritual worlds. The belief that all life was interconnected influenced their social and religious practices, emphasizing harmony with the land and communal responsibility.

6. Celtic Traditions

Agriculture in Celtic Society: The Celts were an ancient European people who inhabited regions that now include Ireland, Scotland, Wales, and parts of France. Their society was heavily agrarian, with agriculture forming the basis of their economy and sustenance. Grain, particularly wheat and barley, was a staple crop.

Deities and Celebrations: Celtic deities such as Brigid and Lugh were celebrated in rituals that emphasized fertility and the harvest. Brigid, associated with fire, healing, and agriculture, was honored during *Imbolc*, a festival that marked the beginning of spring and the preparation for planting. Lugh, connected to the harvest festival *Lughnasadh*, represented skill, craftsmanship, and agricultural prosperity.

Cultural Context: The Celts believed that nature was inhabited by spirits and deities who influenced the cycles of life. Their festivals often involved bonfires, feasting, and the sharing of bread, symbolizing the unity between the people, the earth, and the divine.

7. Native American Traditions

Agricultural Practices: Native American tribes across North America had diverse agricultural practices adapted to their specific regions. For many tribes, maize (corn) was a sacred crop and the cornerstone of their diet and culture. The cultivation of the "Three Sisters"—corn, beans, and squash—was common among many tribes, symbolizing the interconnectedness of life and mutual support.

Spiritual Beliefs: The Corn Mother, a recurring figure in many Native American myths, represents the nurturing and life-sustaining aspects of maize. Harvest celebrations often involved communal feasts, dances, and prayers to express gratitude to the spirits and deities who provided for the people.

Thanksgiving Ceremonies: Tribes such as the Iroquois held ceremonies to give thanks for the harvest and the changing seasons. These rituals often included offerings, songs, and storytelling, reinforcing the importance of gratitude and the cyclical nature of life.

8. Hindu Traditions

Agriculture and Society: Agriculture has been an essential part of Indian society for millennia, with rice, wheat, and millet being the primary crops. Festivals related to the harvest are celebrated with fervor and joy across different states.

Pongal Festival: Pongal is a major harvest festival celebrated in Tamil Nadu and other parts of South India. It is dedicated to Surya, the sun god, and marks the end of the winter solstice. The festival includes the preparation of a dish called *pongal*, made from rice and milk, which is offered to the gods as a sign of gratitude.

Cultural Beliefs: Hindu beliefs emphasize the connection between humans, the earth, and the divine. Festivals like Pongal embody the principles of gratitude, respect for nature, and the celebration of abundance.

9. Japanese Traditions

Agricultural Foundations: Rice has been the staple crop in Japan for centuries, shaping the culture, economy, and religious practices. The cultivation of rice required careful planning, communal effort, and an understanding of natural cycles.

Shinto Practices: The Shinto religion holds that kami (spirits) inhabit all aspects of nature. Rituals like *Niinamesai* involve offering the first fruits of the rice harvest to the kami, symbolizing gratitude and respect for the divine.

Cultural Practices: The emperor's role in conducting the *Niinamesai* ritual signifies the connection between the imperial family, the people, and the gods, emphasizing the belief that agricultural prosperity is tied to spiritual observance.

Conclusion of the Appendix

The diverse cultures and historical contexts outlined in this appendix demonstrate how harvest myths and rituals reflect the relationship between humans and the natural world. These myths are more than stories; they are embodiments of the values, practices, and beliefs that shaped societies. Whether through offerings to deities, communal celebrations, or personal acts of gratitude, these traditions remind us of the interconnectedness of life and the sacredness of the cycles that sustain us.

Understanding the cultural and historical backgrounds of these myths enhances our appreciation of their enduring relevance. They are testaments to humanity's shared experience of nurturing the land, making sacrifices for prosperity, and celebrating the hope of renewal.

Appendix C: Suggested Readings and Resources

For readers interested in further exploring harvest myths, cultural stories, and their relevance across different societies, this appendix offers a curated list of books, articles, and online resources. These suggestions cover various aspects of mythology, cultural history, and the interpretation of agricultural rituals, providing a deeper understanding of the themes and stories discussed throughout this book.

Books on Mythology and Harvest Traditions

1. **"The Golden Bough" by Sir James George Frazer**
   This seminal work is an in-depth exploration of mythology, religion, and folklore across cultures. Frazer's comparative approach provides insights into the shared motifs of sacrifice, renewal, and the cycles of life, making it an essential read for understanding harvest myths and their universal themes.

2. **"Myths from Mesopotamia: Creation, The Flood, Gilgamesh, and Others" translated by Stephanie Dalley**
   This collection offers translations of important Mesopotamian myths, including those related to agricultural cycles and the gods associated with fertility and life. It provides context for understanding how early societies viewed the relationship between the divine and the sustenance provided by the earth.

3. **"Mythology: Timeless Tales of Gods and Heroes" by Edith Hamilton**
   Hamilton's classic book on Greek, Roman, and Norse mythology presents an accessible overview of the gods, goddesses, and heroes. The stories of Demeter, Persephone, and other deities relevant to harvest and renewal are detailed in a way that illuminates their influence on Western culture.

4. **"The Popol Vuh: The Mythic and Heroic Sagas of the K'iche' Maya" translated by Dennis Tedlock**

   The *Popol Vuh* is the sacred book of the Maya, recounting their creation stories and myths of gods, including the Maize God, Hun Hunahpu. Tedlock's translation offers a deep dive into the symbolic importance of maize in Mayan culture and the rituals surrounding it.

5. **"The Complete Gods and Goddesses of Ancient Egypt" by Richard H. Wilkinson**

   This comprehensive resource delves into the deities of ancient Egypt, including Osiris and Renenutet, who were central to harvest myths and agricultural practices. It provides a detailed account of their roles and significance in Egyptian society.

6. **"Pachamama Tales: Folklore from Argentina, Bolivia, Chile, Paraguay, Peru, and Uruguay" by Paula Martin**

   This book offers an exploration of stories and folklore involving Pachamama, the Andean goddess of the earth and fertility. It is a valuable resource for understanding how the Andean people integrated their reverence for the land into their myths and daily lives.

7. **"The Oxford Companion to World Mythology" edited by David Leeming**

   This comprehensive reference book includes entries on various mythologies, gods, and harvest-related rituals from around the world. It is an excellent starting point for readers interested in comparative mythology.

Articles and Academic Papers

1. **"The Cult of Demeter and Persephone: Sacred Rituals of the Eleusinian Mysteries" by Kevin Clinton**
   This article provides an academic look at the Eleusinian Mysteries, which were centered around Demeter and Persephone and their connection to the themes of death and rebirth. It explores the rituals performed and their significance in Greek culture.
2. **"The Significance of Maize in Mesoamerican Culture: An Anthropological Perspective" by Linda Schele**
   This paper examines the importance of maize in Mesoamerican society, including its role in mythology, religious practices, and as a staple of daily life. It highlights the cultural and spiritual symbolism attached to maize and the gods who governed its growth.
3. **"Sacred Landscapes: The Rituals of Pachamama in Andean Cosmology" by Juan Ossio A.**
   This article explores the religious practices and rituals dedicated to Pachamama, focusing on the *Pago a la Tierra* ceremony and its implications for understanding the Andean worldview and reverence for the earth.
4. **"Shinto Rituals and the Symbolism of Rice: An Analysis of Niinamesai" by Noriko Matsumoto**
   An academic exploration of the Shinto harvest festival *Niinamesai*, this paper discusses the symbolic significance of rice in Japanese culture and the ritual practices that honor the kami.
5. **"Lammas and Lughnasadh: Ancient Harvest Traditions and Their Modern Revival" by Caitlin Matthews**
   This article provides an overview of the Celtic harvest festivals of Lammas and Lughnasadh, examining their historical roots and how they have been adapted in modern Pagan and Wiccan practices.

Online Resources and Databases

1. **Theoi Greek Mythology** (https://www.theoi.com/)
   A comprehensive online resource that provides detailed information about Greek gods, goddesses, and mythological stories. The site includes entries on Demeter, Persephone, and other deities associated with harvests and fertility.

2. **Encyclopedia Mythica** (https://pantheon.org/)
   An expansive resource covering myths from various cultures. This site is useful for readers seeking quick references to gods, legends, and mythological terms.

3. **The British Museum Collection Database** (https://www.britishmuseum.org/collection)
   This database includes artifacts related to ancient agricultural practices and religious rituals. It is particularly helpful for visual learners who want to see representations of deities such as Osiris, Ceres, and Pachamama in art and artifacts.

4. **The Smithsonian National Museum of the American Indian** (https://americanindian.si.edu/)
   Offers resources and articles on the agricultural practices and rituals of Native American tribes, including harvest celebrations and their cultural significance.

5. **Maya Exploration Center** (https://www.mayaexploration.org/)
   A valuable source for learning more about Mayan culture, history, and mythology, with specific insights into the role of maize and the importance of the Maize God in their society.

6. **National Institute of Japanese Literature** (http://www.nijl.ac.jp/en/)
   This site provides resources on traditional Japanese literature and

rituals, including academic papers and documents on Shinto practices such as *Niinamesai*.

7. **Internet Sacred Text Archive** (https://www.sacred-texts.com/) A digital library of religious and mythological texts from around the world. This archive includes translated versions of works such as the *Popol Vuh*, ancient Egyptian texts, and other resources related to agricultural myths.

Documentaries and Visual Media

1. **"The Power of Myth" with Joseph Campbell**
   This documentary series, hosted by Bill Moyers and featuring Joseph Campbell, explores the themes of myth in human society. Episodes touch on agricultural myths and their significance across cultures, making it a compelling watch for those interested in understanding the deeper meanings of these stories.

2. **"Legacy of the Gods: The Rituals of Harvest" (National Geographic)**
   A documentary focusing on various harvest rituals around the world, examining their origins, practices, and cultural importance. This program includes in-depth segments on the Eleusinian Mysteries, Mesoamerican maize rituals, and Andean celebrations of Pachamama.

3. **"Mysteries of the Maya" (PBS)**
   This documentary offers insights into the beliefs and practices of the Maya, including their reverence for maize and the role of the Maize God in their agricultural and religious life.

Conclusion of the Appendix

The suggested readings and resources in this appendix provide a pathway for deeper exploration of the harvest myths, deities, and rituals discussed in this book. Whether through scholarly works, engaging documentaries, or comprehensive online databases, these resources offer

further insights into the timeless and universal themes that connect human beings to the earth, the divine, and one another.

Appendix D: Notes on the Poetry

The poetry included throughout this book serves as a reflection and creative interpretation of the themes and stories of harvest myths. This appendix provides insights into the poetic process, interpretations, and the inspiration behind these verses. By understanding the thought and symbolism behind the poetry, readers can gain a deeper appreciation of how these poems connect to the overarching narratives of nurturing, sacrifice, and renewal.

1. The Earth's Embrace

Interpretation: *The Earth's Embrace* is a poem that encapsulates the nurturing aspect of the earth, represented by mother figures like Demeter, Pachamama, and Corn Mother. The imagery of a seed being laid into the soil symbolizes not only the physical act of planting but also the trust and hope embedded in that process. This poem highlights the earth's role as a guardian of life, emphasizing themes of growth, care, and the interconnectedness of all living things.

Poetic Process: The challenge in writing *The Earth's Embrace* was to capture both the simplicity and the profound depth of planting a seed. I focused on language that evokes warmth and nurturing, using words like "cradle," "tender," and "promise" to create a sense of comfort and reassurance. The structure mirrors the cyclical nature of planting and reaping, reinforcing the idea that the earth's care is a continuous and eternal process.

2. Song of the Maize God

Interpretation: This poem draws directly from Mayan mythology, particularly the story of *Hun Hunahpu*, the Maize God who undergoes death and rebirth. The poem reflects the journey through the underworld and the eventual renewal of life, a metaphor for the planting and harvesting of maize. The verses capture the reverence the Maya had for maize as the essence of life and sustenance.

Poetic Process: Writing *Song of the Maize God* involved researching Mayan religious beliefs and their spiritual connection to maize. The poem's cadence was designed to mimic the rhythm of traditional chants, giving it an almost ceremonial quality. I incorporated the motif of fire and darkness to signify the trials faced by the Maize God and the rebirth that follows. The repetition of phrases like "you rose again" is meant to evoke the cyclical theme of renewal.

3. The Cycle of Persephone

Interpretation: *The Cycle of Persephone* delves into the Greek myth of Persephone and Demeter, illustrating the duality of loss and renewal that defines their story. Persephone's descent into the underworld and return symbolizes the cycle of seasons—dormancy followed by growth. The poem explores the emotional weight of Demeter's grief and the joyous resurgence of life with Persephone's return.

Poetic Process: I wanted this poem to capture both the melancholy of winter and the hope of spring. The language shifts from somber to uplifting as the verses progress, mirroring the myth's transition from loss to rebirth. Metaphors like "winter's breath" and "golden light" were chosen to evoke the contrast between cold barrenness and life's return. Structurally, the poem moves from darkness to light, symbolizing the journey from despair to hope.

4. The Feast of Lammas

Interpretation: *The Feast of Lammas* is inspired by the European harvest festival of the same name, which marks the first harvest of grain. This poem celebrates community, gratitude, and the rituals that honor the earth's abundance. The corn dolly mentioned in the poem is a nod to the symbolic figure made from the last sheaf of grain, representing the spirit of the harvest.

Poetic Process: To evoke the communal nature of Lammas, I used imagery of shared meals, singing, and the warmth of togetherness. The structure of the poem is meant to feel rhythmic and celebratory, reflecting the joy and unity that such a festival inspires. Phrases like "first loaf broken" and "songs are sung" are intended to create a sensory experience that invites readers to imagine themselves participating in the celebration.

5. The Dance of Inanna

Interpretation: This poem retells the story of Inanna's descent to the underworld, a powerful Sumerian myth that embodies sacrifice and the promise of renewal. Inanna's journey, during which she surrenders her symbols of power and faces death, is symbolic of planting seeds in the dark soil and waiting for new life to emerge. The poem captures her resilience and the hope that comes from transformation.

Poetic Process: Writing *The Dance of Inanna* required a delicate balance between portraying the starkness of her descent and the triumph of her return. I used strong, vivid language like "gates of stone" and "shadow's grip" to convey the gravity of her journey. The imagery of "new shoots of green" at the end represents the renewal that follows sacrifice. Structurally, the poem mimics a dance, with each stanza representing a step in her journey.

6. Pachamama's Song

Interpretation: *Pachamama's Song* celebrates the Andean goddess Pachamama, embodying her role as a life-giver and protector of the earth. The poem reflects the reciprocal relationship between the people and the land, emphasizing the rituals and offerings made to Pachamama in gratitude for her blessings.

Poetic Process: I wanted this poem to have a harmonious and lyrical quality, akin to a hymn. The use of natural imagery like "mountains, river, and stone" aims to evoke the vastness of Pachamama's influence. The choice of words like "coca leaves" and "chicha" connects the poem to specific Andean traditions, grounding the reader in the cultural practices that honor her. The repetitive structure symbolizes the continuous cycle of giving and receiving.

7. The Offering of Xilonen

Interpretation: Inspired by the Aztec goddess Xilonen, who represents young maize, this poem focuses on themes of sacrifice and gratitude. The poem captures the ritualistic aspects of worship and the deep cultural respect for maize as a life-sustaining crop. It reflects the belief that abundance comes with the price of offerings to appease the gods.

Poetic Process: The tone of *The Offering of Xilonen* is intended to be both solemn and celebratory. I used language that evokes a sense of reverence, such as "drums that echo" and "sacrifice, the blood, the fire," to illustrate the intensity of the rituals. The repetition of Xilonen's name throughout the poem reinforces her importance and invokes the sacredness of her presence.

8. Thanksgiving's Light

Interpretation: *Thanksgiving's Light* draws from Native American harvest traditions that emphasize gratitude and communal sharing. The poem encapsulates the spirit of giving thanks for the land's abundance and highlights the shared experience of coming together as a community to celebrate the harvest.

Poetic Process: This poem was crafted to evoke warmth and a sense of belonging. Phrases like "gathering in the fading light" and "circle tight" are meant to create an image of togetherness around a shared feast. The structure flows like a gentle narrative, guiding the reader through the rituals and emotions associated with thanksgiving and gratitude.

9. The Eternal Dance of Sacrifice

Interpretation: This poem is a reflection on the universal theme of sacrifice in harvest myths. It acknowledges the shared belief that life's cycles are sustained through acts of giving, whether through the selflessness of deities or the hard work of farmers. The poem connects stories of sacrifice from different cultures, illustrating their common thread.

Poetic Process: The verses of *The Eternal Dance of Sacrifice* were designed to feel rhythmic, mirroring the natural cycles of planting and harvesting. I used phrases like "life's roots are cast" and "from death's embrace, the roots will climb" to symbolize renewal emerging from sacrifice. The repetition of the idea of "sacrifice" throughout the poem serves as a reminder of its integral role in sustaining life.

10. The Cycle Unbroken (Final Poetic Reflection)

Interpretation: This final poem ties together the overarching themes of the book: nurturing, sacrifice, and renewal. It serves as a conclusion that reiterates the timeless relevance of these myths, emphasizing that they continue to inspire and teach us about the resilience of the human spirit and the interconnectedness of life.

Poetic Process: For *The Cycle Unbroken*, I aimed to create a sense of continuity and wholeness. The verses are structured to reflect the perpetual movement of time and the cycles that define existence. Phrases like "the myths we tell, the stories spun" and "in every grain and every root" encapsulate the enduring nature of harvest myths and their teachings. The final stanza serves as a call to cherish and honor the wisdom passed down through these stories.

Conclusion of the Appendix

The poetry in this book serves not just as artistic expression but as a bridge between ancient stories and modern interpretation. Each poem was crafted with care to evoke the emotions, imagery, and themes inherent in the myths of harvest and renewal. By understanding the inspiration and symbolism behind these verses, readers can appreciate how poetry breathes new life into timeless stories and offers a fresh perspective on the lessons they impart.

<u>Message from the Author:</u>

I hope you enjoyed this book, I love astrology and knew there was not a book such as this out on the shelf. I love metaphysical items as well. Please check out my other books:

-Life of Government Benefits

-My life of Hell

-My life with Hydrocephalus

-Red Sky

-World Domination:Woman's rule

-World Domination:Woman's Rule 2: The War

-Life and Banishment of Apophis: book 1

-The Kidney Friendly Diet

-The Ultimate Hemp Cookbook

-Creating a Dispensary(legally)

-Cleanliness throughout life: the importance of showering from childhood to adulthood.

-Strong Roots: The Risks of Overcoddling children

-Hemp Horoscopes: Cosmic Insights and Earthly Healing

- Celestial Hemp Navigating the Zodiac: Through the Green Cosmos

-Astrological Hemp: Aligning The Stars with Earth's Ancient Herb

-The Astrological Guide to Hemp: Stars, Signs, and Sacred Leaves

-Green Growth: Innovative Marketing Strategies for your Hemp Products and Dispensary

-Cosmic Cannabis

-Astrological Munchies

-Henry The Hemp

-Zodiacal Roots: The Astrological Soul Of Hemp

- **Green Constellations: Intersection of Hemp and Zodiac**

-Hemp in The Houses: An astrological Adventure Through The Cannabis Galaxy

-Galactic Ganja Guide

Heavenly Hemp

Zodiac Leaves

Doctor Who Astrology

Cannastrology

Stellar Satvias and Cosmic Indicas

Celestial Cannabis: A Zodiac Journey

AstroHerbology: The Sky and The Soil: Volume 1

AstroHerbology:Celestial Cannabis:Volume 2

Cosmic Cannabis Cultivation

The Starry Guide to Herbal Harmony: Volume 1

The Starry Guide to Herbal Harmony: Cannabis Universe: Volume 2

Yugioh Astrology: Astrological Guide to Deck, Duels and more

Nightmare Mansion: Echoes of The Abyss

Nightmare Mansion 2: Legacy of Shadows

Nightmare Mansion 3: Shadows of the Forgotten

Nightmare Mansion 4: Echoes of the Damned

The Life and Banishment of Apophis: Book 2

Nightmare Mansion: Halls of Despair

Healing with Herb: Cannabis and Hydrocephalus

Planetary Pot: Aligning with Astrological Herbs: Volume 1

Fast Track to Freedom: 30 Days to Financial Independence Using AI, Assets, and Agile Hustles

Cosmic Hemp Pathways

How to Become Financially Free in 30 Days: 10,000 Paths to Prosperity

Zodiacal Herbage: Astrological Insights: Volume 1
Nightmare Mansion: Whispers in the Walls
The Daleks Invade Atlantis
Henry the hemp and Hydrocephalus

10X The Kidney Friendly Diet
Cannabis Universe: Adult coloring book
Hemp Astrology: The Healing Power of the Stars
Zodiacal Herbage: Astrological Insights: Cannabis Universe: Volume 2
<u>Planetary Pot: Aligning with Astrological Herbs: Cannabis Universes: Volume 2</u>
Doctor Who Meets the Replicators and SG-1: The Ultimate Battle for Survival
Nightmare Mansion: Curse of the Blood Moon
<u>The Celestial Stoner: A Guide to the Zodiac</u>
Cosmic Pleasures: Sex Toy Astrology for Every Sign
Hydrocephalus Astrology: Navigating the Stars and Healing Waters
Lapis and the Mischievous Chocolate Bar

Celestial Positions: Sexual Astrology for Every Sign
Apophis's Shadow Work Journal: : A Journey of Self-Discovery and Healing
Kinky Cosmos: Sexual Kink Astrology for Every Sign
Digital Cosmos: The Astrological Digimon Compendium
Stellar Seeds: The Cosmic Guide to Growing with Astrology
Apophis's Daily Gratitude Journal

Cat Astrology: Feline Mysteries of the Cosmos
The Cosmic Kama Sutra: An Astrological Guide to Sexual Positions
Unleash Your Potential: A Guided Journal Powered by AI Insights

Whispers of the Enchanted Grove

Cosmic Pleasures: An Astrological Guide to Sexual Kinks

369, 12 Manifestation Journal

Whisper of the nocturne journal(blank journal for writing or drawing)

The Boogey Book

Locked In Reflection: A Chastity Journey Through Locktober

Generating Wealth Quickly:

How to Generate $100,000 in 24 Hours

Star Magic: Harness the Power of the Universe

The Flatulence Chronicles: A Fart Journal for Self-Discovery

The Doctor and The Death Moth

Seize the Day: A Personal Seizure Tracking Journal

The Ultimate Boogeyman Safari: A Journey into the Boogie World and Beyond

Whispers of Samhain: 1,000 Spells of Love, Luck, and Lunar Magic: Samhain Spell Book

Apophis's guides:

Witch's Spellbook Crafting Guide for Halloween

<u>Frost & Flame: The Enchanted Yule Grimoire of 1000 Winter Spells</u>

<u>The Ultimate Boogey Goo Guide & Spooky Activities for Halloween Fun</u>

Harmony of the Scales: A Libra's Spellcraft for Balance and Beauty

The Enchanted Advent: 36 Days of Christmas Wonders

Nightmare Mansion: The Labyrinth of Screams

Harvest of Enchantment: 1,000 Spells of Gratitude, Love, and Fortune for Thanksgiving

The Boogey Chronicles: A Journal of Nightly Encounters and Shadowy Secrets

The 12 Days of Financial Freedom: A Step-by-Step Christmas Countdown to Transform Your Finances

Sigil of the Eternal Spiral Blank Journal

A Christmas Feast: Timeless Recipes for Every Meal

Holiday Stress-Free Solutions: A Survival Guide to Thriving During the Festive Season

Yu-Gi-Oh! Holiday Gifting Mastery: The Ultimate Guide for Fans and Newcomers Alike

Holiday Harmony: A Hydrocephalus Survival Guide for the Festive Season

Celestial Craft: The Witch's Almanac for 2025 – A Cosmic Guide to Manifestations, Moons, and Mystical Events

Doctor Who: The Toymaker's Winter Wonderland

Tulsa King Unveiled: A Thrilling Guide to Stallone's Mafia Masterpiece

Pendulum Craft: A Complete Guide to Crafting and Using Personalized Divination Tools

Nightmare Mansion: Santa's Eternal Eve

Starlight Noel: A Cosmic Journey through Christmas Mysteries

The Dark Architect: Unlocking the Blueprint of Existence

Surviving the Embrace: The Ultimate Guide to Encounters with The Hugging Molly

The Enchanted Codex: Secrets of the Craft for Witches, Wiccans, and Pagans

Harvest of Gratitude: A Complete Thanksgiving Guide

Yuletide Essentials: A Complete Guide to an Authentic and Magical Christmas

Celestial Smokes: A Cosmic Guide to Cigars and Astrology

Living in Balance: A Comprehensive Survival Guide to Thriving with Diabetes Insipidus

Cosmic Symbiosis: The Venom Zodiac Chronicles

The Cursed Paw of Ambition

Cosmic Symbiosis: The Astrological Venom Journal

Celestial Wonders Unfold: A Stargazer's Guide to the Cosmos (2024-2029)

The Ultimate Black Friday Prepper's Guide: Mastering Shopping Strategies and Savings

Cosmic Sales: The Astrological Guide to Black Friday Shopping

If you want solar for your home go here: https://www.harborso-lar.live/apophisenterprises/

Get Some Tarot cards: https://www.makeplayingcards.com/sell/apophis-occult-shop

Get some shirts: <u>https://www.bonfire.com/store/apophis-shirt-emporium/</u>

Instagrams:
@apophis_enterprises,
@apophisbookemporium,
@apophisscardshop
Twitter: @apophisenterpr1
Tiktok:@apophisenterprise
Youtube: @sg1fan23477, @FiresideRetreatKingdom
Hive: @sg1fan23477
CheeLee: @SG1fan23477

Podcast: Apophis Chat Zone: https://open.spotify.com/show/
5zXbrCLEV2xzCp8ybrfHsk?si=fb4d4fdbdce44dec

Newsletter: https://apophiss-newsletter-27c897.beehiiv.com/